"Twenty-seven years ago as a single mom with three small children, no child support, and a job that didn't pay enough to cover child care and health care, I began, finally, to live my life out loud. By harnessing my creative potential I went from a welfare mother to a U.S. congresswoman.

"Everyone is entitled to live his or her life to the fullest. *Living Your Life Out Loud* is full of wonderful commonsense strategies for staying balanced through joy and creativity."

—Representative Lynn Woolsey, U.S. Congress

Joy is a state of mind, and creativity is the critical component to living a joyful life.

The one quality joyful people share is that they know how to express their uniqueness; they sing their own song. We all want to reinvent our lives to live each day more creatively, to be happier and more fulfilled. *Living Your Life Out Loud* is the first and only book that really shows you how to do it.

More than ever, the world needs your creativity and you need to share it with the world. *Living Your Life Out Loud* is about taking action with courage, commitment and boldness. Join the creativity renaissance now—and make your dreams for a joyful life come true.

Padi Selwyn is a professional speaker who is available for conventions, meetings, and conferences. She can be contacted through The Creative Center.

Other Books by Salli Rasberry:

Running a One-Person Business
Marketing Without Advertising
Honest Business
The Briarpatch Book
The Seven Laws of Money
Rasberry Exercises

LIVING YOUR LIFE OUT LOUD

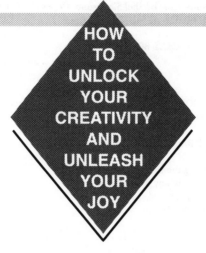

HOW TO UNLOCK YOUR CREATIVITY AND UNLEASH YOUR JOY

SALLI RASBERRY

AND

PADI SELWYN

POCKET BOOKS

New York   London   Toronto   Sydney   Tokyo   Singapore

An *Original* Publication of POCKET BOOKS

POCKET BOOKS, a division of Simon & Schuster Inc.
1230 Avenue of the Americas, New York, NY 10020

ISBN 0-671-89805-1

Cover design by Patrice Kaplan
Text design by Stanley S. Drate/Folio Graphics Co., Inc.

Printed in the U.S.A.

For my daughter, Sasha Marshall: May you continue to live your life out loud and contribute your many gifts to us all.

—SALLI RASBERRY

In loving memory of my Grandma Viola, a creative nurturer whose life was a lesson in the art of compassion and leadership.

—PADI SELWYN

Acknowledgments

To Sasha Marshall, our best in-house critic—thank you, thank you. To our husbands, Reuben Weinzveg and Michael Eschenbach, our thanks for untiring computer troubleshooting and pillow-talk brainstorming, for being our sounding boards and, most of all, our joy buddies.

To our brilliant editor, Tom Miller, who shared our vision and passion and inspired us to surpass ourselves. To Patti Breitman, agent extraordinaire, whose energy and enthusiasm joyfully guided us through the publishing process. To Steve Quirt of Chitra Graphics, for his generous design input.

Hugs to our families and special encouragers—Gail Braverman, Mary Reid, Mirium Redstone, Dorothy Wall, and Susan Page. Special thanks to Phil Wood, Jack Stuppins, Dennis Gillman, Michael Hathaway, and Susan Shaffer for their insights and support.

We are most grateful to Padi's workshop participants, clients and everyone who was interviewed for the book, whom you'll meet in the following pages.

If you ask me what I have come to do in this world, I who am an artist, I will reply: I am here to live my life out loud.

—EMILE ZOLA

Contents

Introduction

There is a vitality, a life force, an energy that is translated through you into action. And because there is only one you in all time, this expression is unique. If you block it, it will never exist through any other medium . . . the world will not have it. It is not your business to determine how good it is, nor how valuable, nor how it compares with other expressions. It is your business to keep it yours clearly and directly—to keep the channel open.

—MARTHA GRAHAM, *Dance to the Piper*

Our culture has traditionally revered musicians, artists, and writers for their creativity. The rest of us have often been left on the sidelines to applaud. If you aren't an artist in the traditional sense, your creativity probably isn't recognized or appreciated. Yet all human beings are designed to be creative and joyful; everyone is born to live his or her life to the fullest, everyone is entitled to the rewards of a creative life. **Creativity is not just for professional artists or wild eccentrics. It is *everyone's* birthright.**

The myth that creativity is just for artists ends here and now. When we speak of creative expression, we mean a life lived creatively, originally, true to one's heart. Creativity is the combination of your life knowledge and your imagination, and it is expressed in forms that are original and of value to you and others. Creativity is a performing art. Having creative ideas is not enough—they must be expressed in a tangible way.

Imagine. Of the nearly six million people on this planet, there is no one like you! No two of us share a common fingerprint. No one has a life just like yours. Just as your fingerprints are unique to you, so is your creative expression.

Creativity isn't just about writing a novel, inventing the microchip, or playing the violin at Carnegie Hall; it's about living your own life out loud. Creative expression comes in many shapes, colors, and sizes. There is no one right way to be creative—the only right way is *your* way.

The difference between creative people and those who are not is purely a matter of self-perception. If you perceive yourself as creative, you are, and if you don't, you won't be.

This book is about perceiving yourself as creative. We offer exercises and inspiration to reinforce what you already suspect—YOU ARE CREATIVE! Then we shine some light on blocks that might be holding you back, on what is keeping you from accessing your creativity and joy. We know it's there. *You* know it's there. It's just a matter of rolling your talents and experiences and unique connections into one pulsating package and expressing yourself in new and meaningful ways. The possibilities are endless once you discover the formula to living a more creative life.

A life creatively lived is a life joyfully lived. Joy is a state of mind. Joy is the essential sense of being connected to the universe. While the subjects of joy and creativity have been covered separately in numerous books, there are no books written specifically about the vital link between them, none that acknowledge that creativity is the critical component to living a joyful, meaningful life. The one overriding quality that joyful people share is that they are living creative lives; expressing their uniqueness, singing their own song. By expressing yourself creatively—through your work, your hobbies, in your personal life and relationships—you, too, can become the joyful, fulfilled person you were meant to be.

Our planet is running out of natural resources. The only resource we have in abundance is human creative potential. Yet few of us know how to mine it for our own joy and the enhancement of all life. *Living Your Life Out Loud* is the book that says (asserts, shouts, screams) that creative expression is necessary for the health of both the individual and the planet.

Writing this book was the most challenging and creative project either of us had ever undertaken. Our personal journeys of growth and discovery have led us to examine our deep-est held beliefs, assumptions, attitudes, and habits. We realized how important the people in our community are to us; their stories are at the heart of this book. Our backgrounds are a crazy quilt of experiences, all of which we tapped into as we created this book. Known as the Entrepreneurial Energizer, Padi co-founded a business bank, hosted a TV show, was presi-dent of an advertising agency, and is a newspaper columnist and international speaker; she has been an entrepreneur since the age of twenty-six. Since the early 1960s, Salli has been a pioneer in the fields of alternative education and values-based business. The author of six books, she cofounded an innovative school and an international network for ethical businesses. A visual artist for over twenty years, Salli sees each day as a blank canvas and is committed to living her life as art.

What we learned from writing this book has changed our lives. During the writing process, we found that our passion for creativity began to permeate every aspect of our lives. We be-gan to push our creative limits, to take more creative risks. As our enthusiasm grew, our work became richer, our daily lives more joyful. We became clearer about our priorities and, as a result, created more balance in our lives.

Because of this, we are committed to bringing joy and cre-ative living out of the closet. Having discovered the vital joy-creativity connection, we have a driving passion to spread the news: Each of us can reinvent our lives to live every day more creatively, fulfilled and happier.

Since 1991, thousands of people across the United States have participated in our creativity programs with life-changing results:

◆ Two hundred workers in a high-tech company spent weeks making masks as a metaphor to acknowledge their creativity. The company now gets hundreds of new ideas each year from people who previously thought they weren't creative.
◆ Managers of a utility company learned to listen and en-courage their co-workers' innovative ideas.

- ◆ Housewives gave themselves permission to rediscover the joys of sculpting, playing the flute, and enjoying interests they had put away after the children came along.
- ◆ Retirees learned that some of the best creative years of their lives were yet to come.

Once you, too, discover the keys to unlock your creativity, you will feel confident, in charge, and more joyful.

Living Your Life Out Loud is a blueprint to help unleash your creative genius; to reclaim your creative birthright, triumph over the Conformity Monster, and feel joyful, confident, in charge, and renewed by the excitement of your endless possibilities. We invite you to join with us in starting a joy and creativity renaissance that celebrates what's good, silly, fun, wild, shocking, lovable, funny, stimulating, and playful about us, the human race. With stories, anecdotes, and easy-to-do exercises, we offer *Living Your Life Out Loud* to guide and inspire you to reconnect with the creative, joyful side of life.

It's time to let joy in and creativity out. So turn the page!

P · A · R · T

ONE

◆

HONORING YOUR CREATIVITY

"I feel like I'm having a love affair with myself."
"Life is a great banquet table and I'm savoring the feast!"

The people who made these statements are not famous, glamorous, or financially rich. They are ordinary people, like us, like you. People you see in the supermarket sniffing the cantaloupes, loading up on paper towels when they're on sale, sneaking a peek at the tabloid headlines as they wait in the checkout line. What sets them apart is that they have discovered the formula for living their lives out loud; they have learned that the path to joy is through creative expression.

If you do not express your own original ideas, if you do not listen to your own being, you will have betrayed yourself.
—ROLLO MAY

Tragically, our social institutions are not designed to encourage creativity or innovation. Instead they often cut us off from our freedom and spontaneity; they successfully trample joy and creativity. What incredible gifts are lost because we fail to nurture and honor each person's unique spirit!

The Conformity Monster

You were born brimming with joy and creative wonder, yet, like most of us, your creativity was probably stifled at an early age by your family and an educational system that believed the only way to make you behave was to make you conform. According to one study, creativity declines when structured education begins. Researcher G. M. Prince found that 90 percent of five-year-olds test highly creative. This drops to 10 percent by age seven, and past age eight only 2 percent exhibit a high level of creativivy.

3

Messages like "Color in the lines," "Now you know, dear, there's no such thing as an imaginary friend," and "Stop making so much racket," taught you that in order to get love and appreciation you had better get in line and fit in. We call this the "Conformity Monster" syndrome.

The Conformity Monster has exacted a heavy toll. By the time many people reach adulthood, they have become separated from their creative essence, never even realizing that this separation may be the cause of the lack of meaning and purpose in their lives.

Until now creativity has never been a focus of society. Our inability to deal effectively with depression, the skyrocketing suicide rates among our nation's youth, homelessness, alcohol and drug addiction, child abuse, spousal battering, and other forms of violence are symptomatic of a joyless culture out of touch with its creativity.

If you aren't acknowledged for being creative, you don't honor your own creativity. When you don't honor your creativity, it withers and wilts like a faded bouquet. Some people are so out of touch with their creative selves that they believe their creativity went the way of crayons and sandboxes.

If you don't feel particularly creative, or creative *enough,* be assured that creativity doesn't die. Dormant creativity is like Rip van Winkle, simply enjoying a long snooze. Just as a muscle that is weak can become strong and useful again, untapped creativity doesn't disappear, it goes underground. Creativity is not a "use it or lose it" proposition.

When you begin to plug into your creativity and start living your life out loud, you not only enhance your creative powers, you begin to fulfill your destiny as a joyful being.

We cannot solve society's problems without beginning with ourselves. We must first unlock our own creativity and set it free. Honoring your creativity is the foundation of a joyful life.

This section explains:

◆ The creative process and how you can use it to uncover your own abundant joy and creativity.

- ◆ The relationship between downtime and uptime and how to foster creativity by taking time out.
- ◆ How to eliminate the nonessentials and hone in on what's important in your life so you can make time for creative expression.
- ◆ How risk-taking builds self-esteem and confidence, prerequisites for living your life out loud.

Although reconnecting with our creativity is not a panacea, the sooner people begin unleashing their creative essence, the better off we will all be. When we make creativity part of our everyday life, we can begin to heal our lives, our communities, maybe even our planet.

As our society becomes increasingly complex, it is more challenging than ever to be joyful. As folksinger and songwriter Buffy St. Marie has said: "You've got to keep your nose to the joy trail." Living a creative life will put you on that trail. Let's begin now; the journey you were destined for, the path of joy and creative expression!

Welcome to the trail head.

The Twelve Traits of Highly Creative People

A first-rate soup is more creative than a second-rate painting.
—ABRAHAM MASLOW, *psychologist*

Each of you has a creative genius locked inside, waiting to be set free. Your potential for creative expression is unlimited, yet most of you use only a tiny fraction of that potential. The more you learn to use your potential, the more you can coax your genie to come out and play, the more joyful your life will be.

Although increasing the amount of joy in your life should be reason enough to unleash that genie, there are many other benefits that come from living your life out loud. Here is a partial list of reasons our many creativity workshop participants over the years have cited for wanting to enhance their creativity:

I want to:

- Have more fun
- Get more control of my life
- Improve my relationships
- Improve my work life
- Enhance my sex life

- Make my dreams come true
- Improve my health
- Feel better about myself (increase my self-esteem)
- Add more zest to my life
- Learn to balance life more effectively
- Make more of a difference in the world
- Express my uniqueness

All of these benefits can be yours, because creativity is like a muscle; the more you exercise it, the stronger it gets. In the next few pages, you are going to learn simple yet powerful ways to exercise your creative muscle. By practicing these traits, you, too, can become more creative. It's not difficult; it just takes awareness and the development of new habits that will serve you well in all areas of your life.

Don't assume our program can't work just because we're not offering any highly complex formulas or asking you to make major sacrifices. Lasting changes come from making small, consistent, manageable changes until they become integrated into your day-to-day life. You definitely don't have to suffer to become more creative and joyful. You've probably suffered enough by keeping your genius locked up for too long already!

EXERCISE

Think of the most creative person you know. List as many adjectives as you can to describe that person.

_____   _____
_____   _____
_____   _____
_____   _____
_____   _____
_____   _____
_____   _____
_____   _____

Let's see how your list compares to ours. From our research and interviews, we have identified twelve characteristics of highly creative people. Of course, not every person has each characteristic in equal amounts, but these are the common attributes they share. The most important thing about this list is that no matter how much of your creative potential you are now using, you can practice these traits and enhance your abilities tremendously.

Traits of Highly Creative People

- Flexibility

- Emotional sensitivity

- Receptivity to new ideas

- Tolerance of ambiguity

- Fluency of ideas

- Preference for disorder

- Intuitiveness

- Originality

- Perseverance

- Openness to risk

- Curiosity (being a "why-ner")

- Playfulness

Let's examine each trait briefly.

Flexibility is critical to creativity because it allows you to change directions easily, and it implies that you give yourself permission to experience new people, places, and things with an open mind. Rigidity is the arch-enemy of your creative genie. Rigid people have hardening of the attitudes! Inflexibility stifles the creative process with an overabundance of judgment before you have even given your ideas a chance.

To practice flexibility, identify something you resist and try exercising this dormant muscle.

For instance, Padi disliked camping. Yet she stopped complaining and started going camping with her family in an effort to be more flexible. A strange thing happened as a result: She found that camping isn't as bad as she thought it would be, and although it will never be her first vacation choice, she learned to enjoy aspects of it. For example, during the campfire, she takes the opportunity to practice her storytelling.

EXERCISE

This exercise is designed to help you identify something you resist or ways you are inflexible that you would like either to change or take a closer look at. Complete the following statement.

Up until today, I have been resistant to:

_____

How does your inflexibility or resistance affect you and others?

1. _____

2. _____

3. _____

4. _____

5. _____

If you were to become more flexible in this area, what could be the major benefits to you or others (i.e., family, co-workers, etc.)

1. _____
2. _____
3. _____
4. _____
5. _____

Ask yourself, "What do I hope to gain by being less rigid about this issue?" Close your eyes, sit back in a comfortable chair, and take a few deep breaths. Imagine yourself doing what you previously would not do. Try to imagine the scene in great detail. Are you alone or with others? If there is conversation, what is being said? What are you feeling about what you are doing? What is the reaction of others? Is it as difficult to be more flexible as you thought it would be?

Salli used this exercise to examine her rigidity around the garden. Her husband really wanted lots of vegetables planted in straight rows like his mother used to have, while Salli insisted on a carefree cottage garden with flowers and vegetables all mingled together. When Michael began to refer to the garden as "her garden," Salli decided to be more open to his point of view before something that was supposed to bring pleasure turned into a contest of wills. Once Salli took a close look at her resistance, she encouraged Michael to plant a few straight rows of onions and garlic. That worked out so well that next year they are going to put in a "traditional" garden adjacent to the existing one. Because of her inflexibility Salli couldn't see the obvious solution until she did the exercise above and she saw the benefits of being more flexible.

> **T**oo many people put off something that brings them joy just because they haven't thought about it, don't have it on their schedule, didn't know it was coming, or are too rigid to depart from the routine. . . . I got to thinking one day about all those women on the *Titanic* who had passed up dessert at dinner that fateful night in an effort to "cut back." From then on, I've tried to be a little more flexible.
> —ERMA BOMBECK

Emotional sensitivity is the ability to feel deeply—your own experiences and those of others. Empathy is important because it deepens connections. This primes the creative pump and opens you up to greater possibilities.

Trying to imagine the reality of others' experiences is something we can all do to open our depths of compassion and understanding.

It's never too early to begin. A very artistic four-year-old boy we know attended a basketball game with his family and found himself standing in line next to a woman with dwarfism. Never having seen a dwarf before, he could hardly take his eyes off her. When his family took their seats in the gymnasium, the boy asked his mother what was wrong with the woman and was given an explanation. Throughout the game, he sat very quietly as if deep in thought. Finally, at intermission, he looked up at his mother and remarked: "I wonder what it feels like to be inside her body."

This kind of empathy and emotional sensitivity comes more naturally to some people than others, but it is a trait that can be cultivated. It is often found in highly creative people, and the ability to capture and communicate it is the source of all great art.

Psychotherapist and corporate consultant Susan Campbell has had a lot of experience with empathy.

> It seems that when people become more emotionally sensitive they also become more connected to their own heart. Opening their heart opens connection to other people. When you feel your own heart . . . your own feelings . . . you enhance your capacity to feel. To feel pain, to feel joy, to feel all the range of human emotions. So you have more access to your own and other people's feelings. You might be stimulated by somebody else feeling something, and that may help you get more in touch with yourself. Or you might be stimulated to have more empathy for some-

body else by going through a crisis or disappointment that connects you with your own feelings more deeply.

I'm thinking of a man I worked with at a large corporation who was real tough and armored until his wife announced that she wanted a divorce. He had thought everything was okay, but they were just going through the motions of marriage. This shocked him into an emotional sensitivity that he'd never felt before. He began to realize that he'd never gotten along very well with his employees either. That he couldn't look them in the eye, and he couldn't listen to their feedback. He could give feedback, but he couldn't receive it from them. His wife's actions shocked him into becoming a more feeling person. Through the course of my coaching him as he went through the divorce, dealing with depression and self-doubts about his management role . . . he turned into a much more real human being.

He decided he wanted to change his management style to be more empathic with his employees, so that he could relate to some of their insecurities, like job insecurity and this kind of thing. Even though his own job was secure, a lot of people under him were afraid of losing theirs. He began to relate more from the feeling part of himself.

One thing led to another, and he actually decided to leave that particular job and take another job within the company that would allow him more chance to be himself. He wanted a fresh start because he was getting to know himself as not such a tough guy and not such a controller. He's working much harder now than he's ever worked before, but he says he's feeling more juice for his work than he ever felt before.

If this is an area you want to stretch in, keeping a journal can help you get more in touch with your feelings—the simple act of writing them down will help you increase self-awareness and understanding. Another way to become more sensitive to others is to practice better listening techniques, such as the ones suggested below.

Listening is hard work. It is a skill that takes a lifetime of practice since it doesn't come naturally. Although we each were given two ears and one mouth so we could listen twice as much as we speak, it rarely works out that way. Becoming a better listener will dramatically improve your relationships with others while helping you develop empathy.

EXERCISE

- ◆ Try waiting two seconds after someone has spoken before you respond. This will help you avoid interrupting and will let others know you want to hear all they have to say. Try to avoid composing your answer while listening.
- ◆ When appropriate, reflect back to the speaker what has been said to make sure you have understood. Use phrases like, "In other words, your chief concern is . . ." or "So, what I hear you saying is . . ."
- ◆ Try to listen for understanding, without reacting or judging. Your own mental chatter often prevents you from really being present with others in conversation because we process information up to ten times the rate of speech, and that leaves lots of time for mind wandering.
- ◆ If you are being asked to listen and are simply too distracted to be truly present with the speaker, say so and arrange another time for the conversation.

Try these techinques by starting with one person in your life with whom you want to improve or enhance a relationship. Make them your listening practice partner. You'll quickly notice a positive change in your relationship by your improvement in listening. This will encourage you to branch out and use these techniques with others regularly.

Receptivity to new ideas is the very foundation of creativity. Be willing to suspend judgment, let go of your assumptions, and stop having to be right every time. This will enable you to open up to new ways of thinking, being, and doing. Pay attention to your inner censor when confronted with new ideas—yours or someone else's. Begin to notice your resistance or receptivity to new ideas. Just the act of becoming aware of how receptive you really are can help you become less judgmental.

EXERCISE

Spend a day paying attention to how receptive you are to new ideas. Monitor your reactions, verbal and nonverbal, to any new idea. On a scale of 1 to 10, how would you rate your receptivity? Do you immediately disregard others' ideas, play devil's advocate (rather than angel's advocate), or really consider what's being suggested? Do you listen without judgment until the idea is explained completely, or do you begin a silent rebuttal until you have a turn to speak?

New ideas are like fine red wine; they need time to breathe. By opening your mind and silencing your voice of judgment, you will encourage the creativity of those around you as well as your own.

Tolerance of ambiguity is a state of mind that gives you the ability to trust that you are creative even when the answers or ideas aren't forthcoming. It means allowing things to remain fuzzy, knowing that it's okay not to know. It's accepting that sometimes your genie needs a little more time to wake up, a little more patient nudging.

It means not panicking when you get stuck. It's being willing to hang out in the unknown—that dark, dank, never-never land of the creative void when you doubt you'll ever have another original idea again.

This is one of the hardest traits to practice because it can be an uncomfortable place to be. All you can do is believe you *are* creative, you *do* have the answers, and they *will* come. After a few episodes of handling ambiguity with trust and patience, you'll begin to know that it's a very temporary state. And the more tolerant and patient you are with yourself, the sooner you are able to move ahead with your creative process, because tolerating ambiguity allows for a greater number of connections with the rest of the universe to be made.

When Padi feels uncertain near deadlines for projects, she uses encouraging self-talk to relax. "I *always* come through and do a great job," she tells herself over and over. Then she thinks of similar situations when she has felt panicked or stuck and remembers that she always does come through—after she's stopped obsessing about it and gotten out of her own way!

To do nothing at all is the most difficult thing in the world.
—OSCAR WILDE

EXERCISE

The next time you find yourself stuck, practice tolerating ambiguity. It's an okay place to be. Simply walk away from the problem. Literally! Go take a walk and change your scenery, or find something else to do that you would find more pleasant. Even taking a refreshing nap or a hot shower can put you in a different state of mind. Know that the answer will come when you stop obsessing about it. Take deep breaths and remind yourself that you have all the answers within yourself.

How do I work? I grope.
—ALBERT EINSTEIN

Fluency of ideas is the ability to generate lots of ideas. It's been said that nothing is as dangerous as an idea when it's the only one we have.

The first ideas you think of are usually the most obvious and least original. When you force yourself to dig deeper, you unearth your creative spirit and begin to generate a more developed level of idea. Highly creative people are comfortable coming up with many ideas and enjoy the process of looking at as many options as possible. When you explore a variety of options, you not only get a better result, you experience a greater feeling of control over the problem.

The best way to practice generating more ideas is to give yourself "idea quotas" when problem solving or developing creative ideas. Don't let yourself stop until you've reached your quota.

This is a practiced skill called *brainstorming*. Brainstorming by yourself or with others can help you strengthen your creative muscle because by juggling the existing patterns you will be generating new ideas. You'll find that very often the *last* ideas you come up with are the most original—the first ideas are usually more predictable.

Brainstorming allows you to piggyback on your ideas or others' ideas, eliminating the unworkable elements and keeping the parts that have value. For example, a manufacturing company held a brainstorming session to generate as many possible solutions as they could to a personnel problem. Their product had to be wrapped in newspaper before shipping, and the assembly line workers were spending too much time reading the paper. As you can well imagine, productivity nose-dived. During the brainstorming session, someone suggested using plain, colored paper to wrap the items, another suggested that foreign language papers might stop the problem, and many other ideas were tossed out. Finally, a frustrated supervisor sitting in the back of the room blurted out: "Why don't we just poke out their eyes?" Everyone giggled nervously until another employee piggybacked on that idea and suggested the solution the company eventually adopted: "Why don't we hire visually impaired workers?"

═══════════════ **EXERCISE** ═══════════════

Describe a problem or challenge you are currently experiencing and have had difficulty resolving:

———————————————————————————————————————

———————————————————————————————————————

Write seven solutions, letting your mind really wander into the realm of the ridiculous. Be as serious or as silly as you want to; don't worry about being practical at this point. Just make sure you come up with seven ideas. Try not to judge the ideas as they come up—don't censor them. Even impractical or socially unacceptable, politically incorrect ideas can lead you to the perfect solution.

1. _____

2. _____

3. _____

4. _____

5. _____

6. _____

7. _____

Most of us look at too few solutions when solving a problem and seize the first plausible idea that comes along. We get lazy and want immediate gratification and results, so we often grab the first, easiest solution off the shelf. Unfortunately, the easy, fast solutions are rarely the most creative or the best. By giving yourself an idea quota, you will expand your mental powers and become a more fluent thinker.

The last key in the bunch is often the one to open the lock.
—ANONYMOUS

Preference for disorder is often evident in messy desks, disorganized closets, and piles of clutter often typify the natural habitat of the creative person, to the chagrin of those who live and work with them. Salli's house, for example, resembles an ongoing craft fair. A twenty-foot redwood slab dominates the living and dining rooms and at any one time might be covered with her husband's blueprints or watercolors, a collage in progress, a square for a group quilt, seeds from the garden, or yarn in heaps waiting to be crocheted into hats. She finds having her projects all around her creatively stimulating and luckily has found a mate who agrees.

Arthur, a friend of ours who is an engineer, was invited to house-sit for his cousin, a noted poet and philosophy professor.

When he and his wife arrived at the empty house, they were appalled at the piles of papers and stacks of books that graced nearly every flat surface of the three-story home. Their house-sitting commitment was for a month, and the couple knew that they wouldn't be comfortable in such chaos for long, so they decided to "clean up the mess," certain that their cousin would be delighted upon his return home. "We believed we were doing him a favor," Arthur explained. "We thought, surely, no one would choose to live this way. He must not have had time to straighten up before his trip." But when the poetic professor returned to his immaculate and well-organized home, he threw a temper tantrum and screamed, "Look at the mess you've made of my house! I'll never find anything ever again!" It was four years until he spoke to his cousin again.

This preference for disorder stems from the fact that highly creative people find it stimulating and challenging to create order out of disorder, sanity from chaos. We don't recommend that you strive to become less organized or sloppier than you already may be, but only want to point out that if you rate an A+ on this trait, it may well mean you're highly creative. So accept your beautiful, messy self and tell those around you how lucky they are to be in your presence.

Since being disorderly takes no great skill, we're not including an exercise here. If you feel compelled to practice, go ahead and mess up your desk or your closet with our blessings!

Intuitiveness is another characteristic of creativity. We all have it, we just don't always use it. And we know that when we ignore it, we get into trouble. The more you can learn to trust your intuition and listen to that tiny voice inside yourself, the more in touch you become with your creative spirit.

Joseph Rafael is a highly acclaimed contemporary American painter currently living and painting in the south of France. Years ago, when he finished an oil painting, he would immediately send it off to his New York gallery, where it would be sold to a collector or museum. After a while, he began to have a strong intuitive feeling that he should keep his work longer before sending it away. This was complicated by the practicalities of cash flow needs, but he was finally able to figure out a system to make it work.

As a result of being able to keep his work longer and study and live with the completed paintings for a period of time, Joseph discovered a new approach to his paintings. His oil paintings, usually done from his photographs, were famous for their translucent, fluid quality. Now, he began painting watercolor renditions of his oil paintings, using his paintings to model from rather than his photographs. As a result, his watercolors reached a brilliant new level of depth and beauty. Recently, he began painting in oils from his watercolors.

This deepening of Rafael's relationship to his own works has greatly affected his style and has led him to a new and exciting relationship to his art, which he may not have discovered had he not listened to his intuition about keeping his work longer. Following his intuition led to an entire new vocabulary in his painting and enabled him to achieve new approaches to his exploration of the qualities of light with which he continually experiments.

EXERCISE

Think about a time when you listened to your intuition and were proven right. What happened?

Think about a time when you didn't listen to your intuition. Why didn't you listen? What happened?

◆ 8 ◆

Originality is the ability to come up with ideas that are new and useful. Here is an example of an original way of looking at our planet.

IF . . .

If the earth were only a few feet in diameter, floating a few feet above a field somewhere, people would come from everywhere to marvel at it. People would walk around it, marveling at its big pools of water, its little pools, and the water flowing between the pools. People would marvel at the bumps on it, and the holes in it, and they would marvel at the very thin layer of gas surrounding it and the water suspended in the gas. The people would marvel at all the creatures in the water. The people would declare it precious because it was the only one, and they would protect it so that it would not be hurt. The ball would be the greatest wonder known, and the people would come to behold it, to be healed, to gain knowledge, to know beauty, and to wonder how it could be. People would love it and defend it with their lives, because they would somehow know that their lives, their own roundness, could be nothing without it. If the earth were only a few feet in diameter.

—ANONYMOUS

Originality can also be enhanced by practice. Inventing or playing with ideas that are new to you gives your brain a good workout and keeps it limber.

EXERCISE

Try challenging yourself with some creative assignments in areas that you enjoy. For example, if you enjoy reading fiction, why not try writing or telling a new ending to the next few stories or books you read? Coming up with alternative captions for cartoons can be a fun exercise. Or play "what if" games with your family and friends. Everyone invents an impossible question and tries to come up with as many answers as possible. What if there were four sexes? What if avocados became illegal? What if animals could speak and humans couldn't? You get the idea!

◆ 9 ◆

Perseverance is fundamental to the creative process because it often takes numerous trials and errors to bring your creations to life. Determination often is what makes a project succeed. When you venture out into new territory, there will always be people who don't support, understand, acknowledge, or agree with you. Unless you are persistent and determined, you can never fully manifest what you want.

We can all take lessons in perseverance from the great inventors. Charles Kettering, one of the most famous industrial inventors of the twentieth century, revolutionized the automobile industry in 1912 with his invention of the self-starting ignition system for the motor car. The difficult and dangerous days of hand-cranked cars were over, making car ownership practical for the masses. General Motors bought Kettering's company, and he headed up their research division for years, bringing to the industry creative innovations such as weather-resistant auto paints and a variety of solutions to mechanical problems. Kettering once said, "An inventor fails 999 times, and if he succeeds once, he's in. He treats his failures simply as practice shots."

Joan Price, writer and exercise trainer, knows a lot about perseverance; it allowed her to transform a nightmare into a very positive turning point in her life.

> I was in an automobile accident where I almost died. I got to the point of seeing the light at the end of the tunnel. I felt I had the option to go or not and decided not to. I had a smashed face. My face had to be reconstructed. I had many, many injuries, and among the worst physically was a shattered heel. The doctor said, "We know we can put you together so you can walk again, but maybe not normally or pain-free," . . . and I replied, "I don't care about walking normally. I want to dance!" I love to move, and I loved to move on my feet. I decided, well, okay, I'll walk with a limp; I don't care, but I'm getting back into my aerobics class.

I was pretty immobile for three and a half weeks in the hospital. I taught myself to walk again literally one step at a time. When they first hoisted me out of the bed and put me on this ramp with railings and said, "Get up," . . . I didn't even have the strength to hold myself up. I would just push myself up out of the wheelchair and sink back into it again.

I would set goals. "The first thing I will be able to do is walk to the nurses' station with crutches and back. Then the next thing is walk around the hospital so much that I become a real bother to everyone and they will send me home. Then the next thing I'll do is learn to walk without my crutches—and so on." Progressive stages. Not the big thing: I will get to this ultimate point. But just: How do I get from where I am now to where I want to be next? Keeping in mind the big picture, but working toward the little step.

I was an English teacher at the time of my accident. Instead of just returning to my aerobics classes, I began teaching exercise. I wanted to share the joy of movement. You don't know how important movement is until you almost can't do it anymore.

Perseverance allowed Joan to dance through life, sharing movement with others instead of being permanently disabled.

EXERCISE

Have you ever given up on a dream or a special goal? In retrospect, do you think you stopped too soon? Do you think you could have succeeded if you had persevered? What kinds of support would you have needed to continue persevering? Under what circumstances would you be willing to try again?

Developing the attribute of perseverance takes practice, but it's habit-forming. Sometimes you just need to believe in yourself a little longer. At other times asking for support from the people who care about you can help you keep going. Pushing yourself past what you think your limits are can be wonderfully exhilarating and eye-opening; you discover how creative you truly are the more you push and persist.

Sadly, many people give up too soon before reaching their goals. Certain goals require years to achieve—because it takes a long time to become masterful in any given field. Nobel-prize economist Herbert A. Simon and his colleagues did some fascinating research into the subject of competence and mastery. They found that nobody reaches world-class status in less than ten years. Their findings were supported by the University of Chicago Development of Talent project, conducted by Benjamin S. Bloom and his associates in 1985. Bloom studied the careers of world-class concert pianists, sculptors, research mathematicians, tennis champions, Olympic swimmers, and research neurologists. He found that unless there is a "long and intensive process of encouragement, nurturance, education, and training, the individuals will not attain world class in their respective fields."

Openness to risk is another obvious trait of highly creative people. It's such an important trait that we've devoted an entire chapter in this book to it. Chapter 4 has an in-depth discussion of this critical characteristic.

Curiosity, or being a "why-ner," characterizes creative doers. We prefer to rename these out-of-the-box thinkers, often labeled whiners, and give them credit for keeping the rest of us on our toes by constantly questioning the status quo. Why-ners can be difficult to work or live with because it seems like they never outgrew asking "why." But that is precisely their magic. They haven't lost the ability to constantly question what the rest of us assume is *just fine the way it is*. That's why why-ners are often great creators and innovators: They're rarely satisfied with what is, and strive to improve upon it. According to Dr.

Marian Cleeves Diamond, brain researcher and professor of Integrated Biology at the University of California at Berkeley, being a why-ner is also good for brain health and vital aging. "One way to be certain of continued enrichment is to maintain curiosity throughout a lifetime. Always asking questions of yourself or others, and in turn seeking out the answers, provides continual challenge to nerve cells," she says.

Asking "why" and "why not" more often can open doors to exciting new realities you may not have considered before. Questioning your assumptions is difficult—if you *knew* what you assumed, you wouldn't assume it! By trying to look at your life and your issues with fresh eyes, and asking "why" more often, you can begin to seek better ways of doing everything.

EXERCISE

We all get used to doing things a certain way. This can create ruts, which keep us from enjoying our lives to the fullest. The questions below may ask you to challenge some of your assumptions. Take a few minutes to think about each one; you may even enjoy discussing some of them with your friends, family, or co-workers.

◆ Why not live abroad in a radically different culture for a year?
◆ Why not go back to school and get another degree or study a new subject?
◆ Why not plan an entirely new career?
◆ Why not learn to play a musical instrument (or another one)?
◆ Why not begin to draw or paint?
◆ Why not move all the furniture to new places in your house?
◆ Why not start dressing like your fantasy-self would?
◆ Why not buy presents for people when it's not their birthday?
◆ Why not call up someone you admire but have never met?
◆ Why not whisk your partner away for a weekend planned by you?
◆ Why not have a picnic using your best china and a fancy tablecloth?
◆ Why not have a real tea party with a three-year-old?
◆ Why not contact someone you haven't seen in many years?

Once you have thought about the "why nots" above, make a list of five of your own "why nots." Put this list on your refrigerator or somewhere else where you will see it often. Consider doing some or all of them.

Playfulness is another trait so vital that we've devoted Chapter 12 to it. Through play, you let down your defenses, reduce the stress that blocks creativity, and let a more spontaneous side of yourself break free.

EXERCISE

You probably already have several of the twelve traits of highly creative people. Look over the list on page 9 again and rate yourself between 1 and 5 for each trait, with 1 being the lowest score and 5 being the highest. This will help you determine which traits you need to work on to enhance your creative abilities as well as celebrate the attributes you have.

Which of these traits come easily to you? Which ones need the most work? Remember that creativity is a muscle—the more it's exercised the stronger it gets.

◆ By practicing and acknowledging these twelve traits, you begin to nurture your creative spirit. When you give yourself room to grow in these new and exciting ways, you honor yourself in the most loving and validating ways possible. You take an important step—you begin living your life out loud.

2

Quantum Creativity

The creative process is as natural as breathing. We all use it, but most of us aren't even aware of it. It's subtle, mysterious, and happens on a subconscious level. The trick to boosting your joy and creativity is to make it happen on a conscious level.

When we consciously commit to enhancing our creativity, then can we begin to tear down self-imposed barriers and maximize our endless creative possibilities. Quantum creativity is the capacity we each possess to surpass ourselves—to go beyond our former limits, to exceed our highest self-expectations by continually setting new standards of performance. You experience quantum creativity when you realize your creative potential is limitless in any area you wish to pursue.

Once you become aware of the four easy steps you are already using, you can begin to consciously plug into and harness your creativity. Whether you are wrestling with a life challenge, seeking the inspiration for an original new creation, or just trying to have better ideas more consistently, the process described below is simple, yet powerful. It has been used by creativity researchers for decades and is now available to you! These four steps of the creative process were first identified in the late nineteenth century by the German physiologist and physicist Hermann von Helmholtz and later expanded upon in 1926 by Graham Wallas in *The Art of Thought*.

The Four Steps of the Creative Process

1. Preparation
2. Incubation
3. Illumination
4. Verification

Preparation

Preparation is the first phase of the creative process. Preparation includes your education and experience regarding the problem you are trying to solve or the creation you are trying to birth. For example, if you were faced with designing and creating the prehistoric effects (including a twenty-foot, ten-thousand-pound *Tyrannosaurus rex*) for the movie *Jurassic Park,* you might do what associate producer Lata Ryan and crew did. Since nothing had ever been attempted like this on such a huge scale, they started by watching *every* dinosaur movie ever made. Next they pulled together experts in the field. They then made fifth-scale models for Steven Spielberg's approval, including built-up computer-generated dinosaurs, before moving on to create full-sized species of dinosaurs. They would build something, try it, and modify it until it was right. These steps would all help prepare you, as they did Ryan's crew, to design a superior replica of a *Tyrannosaurus rex* or *Dilophosaurus;* and your ability to be successful would be determined to a large extent on how well you prepared yourself with information before tackling the problem.

Incubation

Incubation, the second phase in the creative process, is when the magic of creativity transforms the raw material of preparation and begins to percolate on an unconscious level, so the new idea can surface. Incubation is the critical process of letting the problem go, putting it on the back burner, and delegating the problem to your subconscious mind. It gives your conscious mind a rest from what you've been working on, and it provides an opportunity to quiet the incessant internal chatter.

We refer to incubation as "time out." The value of time out in liberating creativity cannot be overstated. Taking time out is a prerequisite for reaching new creative heights and fuller self-expression. Incubation is downtime, and downtime is necessary for quantum creativity. We'll discuss downtime in greater depth in the next chapter.

Most of you have experienced the natural phenomenon of waking up in the middle of the night with the solution to a problem, or getting a brilliant flash of insight while driving, taking a shower, or jogging. When you get that flash while involved in another activity—at unexpected moments when doing something completely unrelated to the problem you are trying to sort out—this is incubation at work. Incubation is the answer to Albert Einstein's rhetorical question, "Why is it I always get my best ideas while shaving?"

History is full of examples of creative geniuses and the role of incubation. Einstein, for instance, came up with the theory of relativity while sitting on a hillside imagining himself riding upon a sunbeam. Newton was daydreaming under an apple tree when he formulated the laws of gravity. Descartes invented analytical geometry while watching a fly crawl on a wall. George Washington was watching the rain from a cabin in the woods when the vision of America's future appeared to him.

Some peak creative performers have attempted to describe the magical incubation experience. Mozart wrote in a letter dated 1789:

> When I am . . . completely by myself, entirely alone, and of good cheer, say, traveling in a carriage or walking after a good meal, or during the night when I cannot sleep; it is on such occasions that my ideas flow best and most abundantly. Whence and how they come, I know not; nor can I force them.

Mozart would "receive" entire musical compositions, which were perfect and needed only to be written down.

The experience of channeling works of written, musical, or visual art are common among people in touch with the power of incubation, who let themselves take the time to nurture this powerful process.

To Rudyard Kipling the key to gaining access to his "inner helper" was "not to think consciously, but to drift. Drift, wait, and obey," he recommended.

James Watson and Francis Crick, the scientists who discovered DNA, wrote: "Much of our success was due to the long, uneventful period when we walked around the colleges or read the new books."

Walking around, shaving, taking a shower, and even doing something as ordinary as driving can prompt creative ideas. Kelley, a professional corporate trainer, found that driving is a powerful way to let part of her mind drift off and sift through all her stored images until a perfect solution appears.

"I've programmed myself to use driving time as incubation time," she explains. One day a client called to discuss a workshop Kelley was planning and told her that he needed the title of her program—in fifteen minutes. Sitting at her desk racking her brain proved fruitless as the time ticked away. Having just a few minutes left, she decided to jump in her car for a creative ride around the block. As soon as she put the key in the ignition, the perfect title popped into her head: "Take This Job and Love It: Self-motivation for Managers."

Joyce Wycoff, author of *Mindmapping,* used her awareness of the power of the creative process to help launch an exciting new endeavor in the field of creativity.

> We were in Delta's Crown Room at the Los Angeles Airport kicking around ideas about possible training programs when the idea surfaced to create an association of people interested in organizational learning and thinking.
>
> It was an idea that had been popping up for me on occasion over the past six or seven years. Although there were a couple of existing creativity associations, their primary focus seemed to be academic research and individ-

ual creativity and they were lacking in any business and organizational focus.

A technique I had discovered years before as a way of verifying new ideas was to put them away in a mental box. If I reopened the box later and the idea was bigger and brighter, it was probably a good one. When the association idea came out of the box again at the airport meeting, it was definitely bigger and brighter. It started building on all the years of preparation and incubation, and by the next day it had claimed a name for itself . . . the Innovative Thinking Network.

Call it tapping into the collective unconscious, calling your guardian angel collect, unleashing the genius inside, harnessing your inner mentor, digging deep into your unconscious mind—whatever you call it, it will work for you.

Incubation has been compared to composting. When you compost, you basically throw organic waste (food garbage or garden clippings) into a pile and let it rot for a while. You leave it alone and come back to find garbage transformed into incredible, fertile soil that stimulates your garden to grow to new heights of health and beauty. By letting go and walking away from your mental "pile of garbage," you will discover a garden of great ideas sprouting from your mind.

Another creative incubator, D. Wayne Silby, founder and chairman of the board of the Calvert Group of Investment Funds, said, "Often we have the answers to our problems, but we don't quiet ourselves enough to see the solutions below the surface." Obviously a man who walked his talk, Silby's business card used to read "Chief Daydreamer."

Scientific research sheds new light on the importance of unplugging. Psychologist Burton White of Harvard University's Child Development Center found that one in thirty children could be described as "happy and brilliant." Research was conducted to find out what demographic or psychological factors they shared. Professor White found out that these children only had one thing in common: All spent noticeable amounts of time staring peacefully and wordlessly into space every day.

The best times to take time out are when you are tired, distracted, feeling stressed, or simply stuck in your creative process. But you need not wait until you've reached the end of your mental rope to take a break. Getting into the habit of taking time out will increase your overall benefits because the entire creative process will become more natural and comfortable for you.

Screenwriter and director Eugene Core takes time daily for what he calls "chair and stare" time—time to just sit and do nothing at all, to quiet his mind so that the images and ideas that will later appear in his films can bubble up to the surface and speak to him.

Illumination

At last! The payoff! The third step in the creative process is Illumination, that moment an idea or solution explodes into your mind. It's the Aha! stage when the perfect answer arrives seemingly out of nowhere. This explosion can come at any time, but most often appears during periods of downtime or shortly thereafter. Some experts believe this occurs on an awareness level suspended between the conscious and unconscious minds. Carl Jung called the awareness level "Primordial Mind"; others called it reverie.

It's important to keep paper and pencil or a tape recorder handy so you can catch these great ideas and insights. You've probably experienced having a wonderful idea or insight while driving or upon waking, only to have it fade away because you didn't write it down. You were so sure you would recall it, and then, like a delicate, elusive butterfly, it disappeared.

Make sure you don't let your great ideas get away.

Paul is an engineer who has a terrific way of recording the cascade of ideas he receives in the middle of the night. He has programmed the telephone on his nightstand to speed-dial his voice mail at work, so with the simple push of a button, he can record his brainstorms in the middle of the night. When he arrives at work in the morning, he replays his creative flashes.

It's especially important to keep idea recording tools beside your bed. Waking time and drifting off to sleep time are very fertile grounds for creative ideas. Researchers have found that major insights are more likely to take place when brainwaves are in the theta or alpha range. These lower frequencies and higher amplitudes blend together those creative ideas bubbling up to the surface. This explains why inventors like Thomas Edison got some of their best ideas following catnaps. Napoleon and Winston Churchill also attributed their dynamic performance in part to daily naps. President Bill Clinton is known for dozing off after wrestling with a brain-crunching problem, to awaken with the answer.

> John D. Rockefeller's incredible wealth, and longevity—ninety-eight years—owe something to his daily incubation periods. He attributed his long life span in part to taking a half hour nap every day at noon. Another napper, Henry Ford, lived to be eighty-four and was known for his enormous energy. His formula: "I never stand up when I can sit down, and I never sit down when I can lie down."

Many people experience this heightened creative awareness just before drifting off to sleep. Sleep researchers call this the hypnogogic state, when our mental images are a mixture of dream pictures and conscious thoughts. The hypnopompic state is the one you enter upon waking up, when the brain is in the theta wave stage, also filled with a mixture of dream and controlled images. Both these stages are like trance states and have been called the gateways to creativity. The next time someone disturbs you when you're in this magical mind-frame, tell them you're hypnogoging or hypnopomping, and they'll surely leave you alone.

Did the Spaniards know more than they were letting on when they said, "How beautiful it is to do nothing and then rest afterward"? Perhaps they knew that resting and drifting off also encourage great ideas to flow. One thing is for certain—nothing feels quite as beautiful as a problem solved or a creative idea born.

Verification

The last stage of the creative process is Verification and simply involves trying out the solution and making sure it works. This is the time to fine-tune ideas for enhancement or revision; brainstorm with others and try out your idea. But most of the ideas received are perfect, and you have only to trust in them and give them a try. Sometimes ideas need time to ripen, however, so you may need to sit with the information you receive until you feel ready to take action.

Some ideas can take years to come to fruition. After six years of incubation Joyce Wycoff verified her idea for the Innovative Thinking Network by faxing a questionnaire to thirty associates who were interested in creativity and innovation in organizations to assess their interest and ask for potential support. The response was overwhelmingly positive, and within six weeks of the airport meeting, the Innovative Thinking Network had a board of advisors and began accepting members.

By consciously tapping into this simple four-step process for quantum creativity, you, too, can increase your creative output. When you consciously prepare, incubate, trust that illumination will come, and then verify, you can consciously plug into your powers and unleash your creative genius. Make it a priority and you'll make it happen.

3

Balancing Uptime, Downtime, and the 10% Solution

It doesn't seem fair. The only socially sanctioned call for "time out" is reserved for coaches during sporting events or children needing to take a break in the midst of playtime's wild abandon. Yet nobody needs time out more than people wanting to fill their lives with abundant joy and creative expression.

Taking time out is one of the most powerful ways you can honor your creativity.

It is impossible to experience joy fully if you are flipping rapidly through the datebook of life. As you check off endless appointments, there is little time to feel much of anything. Joy and creativity go into hibernation like weary, lumbering bears, hopefully to reappear when the ground thaws and the climate changes. If you want your joy and creativity to come alive, it's up to you to change the climate.

Researcher and author Charles Garfield discovered that peak performers typically have a pattern of tremendous productivity followed by periods of downtime to recuperate and reenergize before harnessing another surge of creative energy. Every great performer, from athletes to dancers, speakers to singers, teachers to actors, require time to wind up and wind down. No one can maintain maximum output, full speed ahead, all the time. If you are not savoring your life and if you feel like a windup toy that's wound too tightly, it's time to put more downtime into your life.

The human body was not designed to go nonstop day after day, month after month, without time out. Notice how many people get sick and then openly admit, "I guess my body was telling me I needed a rest, and this is the only way I could get it." How sad to have to get sick before you are willing to admit you need to slow down and recharge yourself.

Unless you build pauses and renewal time into your daily life, your body will continue shouting for time out until it just gives out, forcing you to sit up and take notice in a major way.

Highly creative achievers make time for themselves a priority, because they know, consciously or intuitively, that recharging the creative batteries happens during downtime. Getting in touch with your inner rhythm is critical to creative health.

Sara Alexander, artist and psychotherapist, has structured her life so that she has her mornings for quiet and creative time and then in the afternoon sees her clients.

> I usually wake up and go for a walk with friends, or I spend half an hour in the garden. I do something outdoors in the beginning of every day. Then I write at my desk for an hour or work on my furniture assemblage. I refurbish old furniture, junk furniture from thrift stores and garage sales. I usually sand off the paint partway and patchwork different pieces together with the help of my friend who is a carpenter. Or I might work on a collage using bits of old paper . . . ribbons . . . dried roses, feathers, seashells, whatever I happen to find. I might make some creative decision about my clothing or my house. I see my psychotherapy clients in the afternoon, which means I have the morning for myself.

If getting rid of stress is not enough incentive to motivate you to take more time out, consider this—we each have only so much time left on the planet. We are used to thinking of our time as if it will never run out, and we speak in vague, broad terms such as "My life is half over" or "I have my whole life

ahead of me." When you begin thinking of your life in increments of hours and days, however, time takes on an entirely
different dimension.

Salli recently ran into a politician friend at the opera who
was looking particularly harried. Instead of ignoring her
friend's stress, Salli asked what was going on.

"Oh, everything is falling apart—there is just too much to
do and I can't hold it all together, but someone has to try."

Salli looked her friend in the eye and asked, "If you had ten
days or two hundred and forty more hours to live, what would
you do?"

"I'd try to enjoy them," Bette whispered. "I never really
thought of it like that."

Realistically, unless time out is programmed into every day,
it's tempting to fall into the trap of being a busy-addict; constantly on the move, harried, and on autopilot. Our society rewards Superman and Superwoman (translation: overbooked
and still smiling), and as a result almost everyone has a major
struggle with balancing downtime and uptime. Downtime will
initially take planning and discipline until it becomes a habit.
In a relatively short time, however, you will begin to experience
the pleasures and benefits of taking time out without needing
to break down.

We are not suggesting that you ignore your responsibilities
or duck difficult situations, but we do want to encourage you to
pay attention to your unique downtime-uptime rhythms so that
you can enjoy a more balanced and creative life. Instead of
sharing stress stories with your friends, you will soon be sharing joy.

Hanging out was once a natural state of being—politically
correct, socially sanctioned. Yet sadly, it's become a lost art for
most of us. Salli wrote the following piece, which first appeared
in the twenty-year-anniversary *Whole Earth Review*, recounting
how and why she revived this lost art in her life.

It was thought I had a brain tumor. My closest friends
came to visit me; flowers and love and tears filled my tiny
hospital room. I was one of the few patients with a private

room. By the second day I was feeling frail. The signals were strong. This was it. Or worse, this wasn't it, and I would linger on for months, tested and retested while my friends debated when to pull the plug.

Actually it was a mysterious virus that had invaded my body. I sure do love that virus. That little beastie offered me an opportunity to take a good look at what is important. My visitors were actually taking time away from their work. I was amazed and very touched. We were sharing whole afternoons! We weren't accomplishing anything! I felt guilty. I felt great.

Shortly after my hospital experience, a friend whipped out her minute-by-minute planner stating, "I'll pencil you in." I was shocked. Being penciled in meant I could be *erased!* I realized just how shaped we had become by those books. Without them would our lives flow a bit too much?

I now spend a quarter of my time with friends and family. I am almost single-handedly attempting to revive the lost art of "hanging out" and spontaneity. And you know, it's been wonderful. Not one person has refused the invitation to just be together for a few hours. No agenda, no destination. The few that have hesitated quickly give in when asked if they would take the time to attend my funeral.

EXERCISE

During the next week, keep a personal rhythm log and record the times of the day you feel:

◆ Most energetic
◆ Least energetic
◆ Inspired and creative
   If the last one seems difficult to do, try this focusing tip. In your log write down: How many uses can I think of for one hundred Ping-Pong balls? Whenever you get an idea about that particular action, write it down and log in the time you had the idea. You will find that there are certain periods each day when you'll generate many ideas. This is the time to note as your most productive, creative time.

With this exercise you'll discover a pattern, and it may surprise you. When Padi began paying attention to her rhythms several years ago, she discovered that her most creative ideas came to her in the middle of the night—usually around 3:00 A.M. Armed with this insight, Padi now awakens for a few hours each night to harvest ideas during this fertile, creative time. Not surprisingly, a few days each week, she'll take naps in the early afternoon to catch up on sleep. As a result of tuning in to her own inner rhythm, she is more productive and her creative output has improved.

> **M**ay you live all the days of your life.
> —Old Irish Proverb

When you measure the time you have allotted to you by hours and days, every minute suddenly seems more precious. Just the exercise of reading the actuarial chart below can be enriching. If you are like most people, you probably avoid

IF YOU ARE	Yrs.	THIS IS THE ESTIMATED AMOUNT OF TIME YOU HAVE LEFT		
		Total Hrs.	Waking Hrs.	Days
20 YEARS OLD	55.7	481,248	360,936	20,331
25	51.0	440,640	330,480	18,615
30	46.3	400,032	300,024	16,900
35	41.6	359,424	269,568	15,184
40	37.0	319,680	239,760	13,505
45	32.5	280,800	210,600	11,863
50	28.1	242,784	182,088	10,257
55	24.1	208,224	156,168	8,797
60	20.2	174,528	130,896	7,373
65	16.7	144,288	108,216	6,096
70	13.5	116,640	87,480	4,928

thinking about how much time you have left, as if the very thought might somehow diminish your life. Actually, the reverse is true. When people in our creativity classes begin to closely examine how they spend their time and consider the hours, days, and years ahead, they come to terms with their values and priorities. They begin asking important questions such as, "At what pace do I want to live my life? How do I choose to spend the rest of my time here? What can I eliminate from my life to create more room for joy and creative expression?" Scheduling downtime and uptime suddenly makes good sense.

Tibbets Woodworking in Windsor, Massachusetts, sells custom-made "Life Coffins," ranging from $365 to $505, which they suggest using as a bookcase or for wine storage until your funeral. Their brochure explains: "Why would anyone buy a Life Coffin? Death is an inevitable part of life. Buying a coffin now can help begin a process of education and acceptance: By seeing your coffin every day, you will be reminded of the preciousness of your physical life. This perspective on your daily hassles can bring you to celebrate the miracle of life."

The following is a humorous German story about life and the quality of time.

THE LENGTH OF LIFE

When God was finished creating the world, the time came to fix the length of each creature's life. One by one, the animals came to Him to discuss the matter.

The donkey was the first to appear and ask God how long his life would be.

"Thirty years," replied, God. "Does that please you?"

"Oh, dear God," whined the donkey, "that is an awfully long time. What a painful existence to carry heavy loads from morning till night for all those years. Please don't let me suffer so long!" Well, God took pity on him and relieved him of eighteen years, and the donkey left feeling comforted.

Then the dog appeared, and God offered him thirty years, too.

"Lord," pleaded the dog, "Think about how I shall have to run till my feet fall off, my bark could never last that long, nor my teeth for biting." Seeing he was right, God relieved him of twelve years and sent him off.

Then the monkey arrived. "You'll want to live thirty years, won't you?" asked God. "After all, you carry no heavy burdens or work like the dog—you just play." But the monkey declined the generous life span, too, saying he was always the brunt of jokes, teased by children, and thirty years of that was too much for him to stand.

At last, man appeared, joyful, energetic, and vigorous. "Thirty years you shall live," proclaimed God. "Is that sufficient?"

"What a dreadfully short time," cried man. "When I have built my house, raised my family, when I have planted trees that blossom and give fruit, and am just starting to enjoy my life, I will die? Oh, please give me more time here on earth!"

"I will add to it the donkey's eighteen years," agreed God.

"That is not enough," begged man.

"All right. You shall also have the dog's twelve years."

"Not long enough!"

"Well, then," replied God, "I will give you the monkey's ten years also, but more you shall not have." The man went away, but was still not satisfied. So man lives seventy years. The first thirty are his human years when he is healthy, merry, and works joyfully. Then follow the donkey's years, when burden after burden are laid upon him. Then come the dog's twelve years, when he growls and has no teeth to bite with. And when this time is over, the monkey's ten years from the end. Then man is weak-headed and foolish, doing silly things and becoming the jest of children.

—Adapted from *A Treasury of Jewish Folklore* by Nathan Ausubel (Crown Publishers, 1955)

Guard the senses and life is ever full . . . always be busy and life is beyond hope.

—LAO-TZU

The 10% Solution

One excellent way to begin to manage the downtime/uptime dilemma is to acknowledge your priorities. Many of us go through life without expressing our priorities even to ourselves, tending to take for granted what we hold most dear. For instance, we ignore our bodies, assuming "if it ain't broke, don't fix it," or that we can keep adding on more and more commitments, or that our friends and family will always be there for us.

To remain clear about priorities, we use the 10% Solution developed by Gudrun Cable, a mother and owner of two successful businesses.

Gudrun's formula helps to clarify values by weeding out the nonessentials, and facilitates the communication of priorities with family and others. We all have 100% to deal with in our lives: 10% is important, 90% unimportant. The secret to a happy, productive life is to deal with the 10% and let the 90% slip.

> **K**now what's important to you. Ask yourself what really matters in your relationships, your work, and for you individually. Then ask yourself: "Do I spend my time on things that really matter to me? Or do I spend time on other people's goals?" ... There are three small two-letter words that are essential to survival in the nineties: NO, NO, and NO. It's okay to say NO! You cannot and should not do everything that everyone asks you to do. Many people have the notion that it is wrong to turn someone down. I used to feel that way, but I found out that I started to hate the pace of my life. Burned-out people are of little value. Say NO to the things that are not consistent with the goals you have for your life.
>
> —DANIEL G. AMEN, *psychiatrist*

Gudrun has lived by the 10% formula for over ten years and devotes as much of her energy and time as possible to her 10%. She has a full, rich life that even includes time for driving friends to doctors' appointments, picking them up at the airport, and just hanging out with the people in her 10%. Owner of the Sylvia Beach Hotel, a haven for booklovers located on the Oregon coast, Gudrun is an avid reader, and meeting authors she admires is also in her 10%, which is how she came to meet Salli. Salli remembers:

> When Gudrun learned that I was coming to Portland to meet with a well-known healer, she called, introduced herself, and immediately invited me to be her guest at the

hotel, where each room is fashioned after the period and style of a famous author. "No phones, no television, no interruptions, and the entire upper floor is filled with books and lots of comfy chairs and sofas," Gudrun promised. The only hitch was that the hotel was 125 miles from the doctor's, and I was unable to drive. "Not to worry," said Gudrun, "I will come and get you, drive you to your doctor's appointment, wait for you, and then drive you up to the hotel and make sure someone drives you to the airport in time to catch your flight home. We will have a great time," she added. And that's how I learned about the 10% Solution.

The 10% Solution renders decision making easy. For example, included in Gudrun's 90% unimportant category are washing her car, reading the newspaper, watching television, gossiping, having ceremonial conversations (trite small talk, in her vernacular), maintaining a diverse wardrobe, and having her nails done. "In freeing yourself from things that don't matter to you, you can put full effort into the things that do," Gudrun points out.

Once when she and her daughter were on the freeway during rush hour, a man ran into them, putting a dent in her new Honda. Assured no one was hurt, she just got back in her car and drove on her way. Her daughter was incredulous; her mom had not even gotten the other driver's insurance information. To this day Gudrun smiles. "It's just not in my 10%."

And what has Gudrun sacrificed as a result of ignoring the 90%? She has a dirty car until it rains, which is frequent in Oregon, anyway. She doesn't know what David Letterman or Jay Leno said to his guest last night and couldn't care less about flaunting the latest fashions. Deprived? She doesn't know what the word means in relation to her own life!

By continually focusing on your priorities, you can become increasingly discriminating about how you spend your time, which is, of course, how you spend your life. And you will begin to create the time you need to unplug, relax, and incubate your way toward greater creativity and joy.

EXERCISE

What is in your 10%? What's in your 90%? Make as long a list as you can for each category. Share your list with family and friends. (Only if they're in your 10%, of course!) This is a wonderful ritual to begin the new year with, or a great annual birthday exercise. But don't put it off until then. Do it now, and then repeat the exercise at least twice a year, since your 10% and 90% categories will probably change.

===

Refer to your 10% and 90% often. You'll make it easy for your family and friends to support your priorities and find it's a great way to communicate what's important to you. When your priorities change, it won't be a secret to those near and dear.

Salli used to work full tilt, without a pause to savor her accomplishments. She would finish one book and without missing a beat begin working on the next one. Several years ago she reevaluated her priorities and work rhythms, and now when she finishes a big project she takes at least a month off to enjoy long walks with friends, visit art galleries, try new recipes, take classes, and in general enjoy her life. Salli now returns to her work full of zest, with her creative batteries fully charged.

> **Y**our children, when grown, won't remember how clean the house was. But they will remember how you looked when you smiled and the sound of your laughter, long after you're gone.
>
> —SHIRLEY SOILEE

Your natural rhythm is as unique as you are. When you tune into your rhythm, you will learn how best to use your time. Remember, how you spend your time is how you spend your life, and learning about your own rhythm will help you spend it more wisely and joyfully.

> **S**aying no, an essential part of keeping your priorities in focus, can be an art. Wendell Berry, farmer-poet-economist-author, uses the following rejection letter to decline unwanted requests or invitations that are not in his 10%.

Dear Friend,
Your kindness deserves a better fate
This reply is probably already late,
And would be later if I didn't have it thus printed out.
Such promptness is nothing to brag about;
It is just the best I can do,
Since I am (like, undoubtedly, you)
Too busy, which is bad manners and a poor excuse.
But I'm resigned, I regret to say, to this abuse
Of courtesy, and to doing part of my duty
By neglecting the rest. The beauty
Is in the part I do;
The neglect, I guess, is only true.
But some things I don't do anymore,
And some things I never did before
I still don't do. I don't talk on TV
Because I don't like mechanically enforced stupidity,
But aside from its falsehood and its tedium
I just don't trust the damned medium.
I rarely have time to read unpublished books;
I read too few published ones. And it looks
As if I had better say too
That I don't know which magazines will publish you
Or me. And I never give advice
To anybody who may be so nice
As to take it. I can't edit poems, interpret Scripture,
Or go anywhere to give a lecture.
I hate travel by Interstate and travel by air.
I'm almost not going anywhere.

A bird who cannot fly and sing,
I'm almost not doing anything
That can't be done at home. To your health,
Friend! Try staying home yourself.

4

Risk to Grow

Alas for those that never sing, but die with all their music in them.
—OLIVER WENDELL HOLMES

Life is about taking risks. More than any other factor, the willingness to risk will determine your ability to liberate your creative genius and find joy. It is only through taking risks that you push beyond your greatest expectations, surpassing your hopes and dreams. Padi says:

> After I had been in the advertising business for thirteen years, I began to feel the need to do something else. The lack of client and employee loyalty inherent in the ad game began to wear me down. At the same time, my second son had just been born, and the stress of mothering two children while running a fifteen-employee company that I no longer felt good about was making me ill. I landed in the hospital with piercing chest pains and ended up with a chronic digestive problem. For several months after my release from the hospital, every Monday morning before leaving for work, I vomited.

46

For a while I thought I was on automatic pilot from a few years of morning sickness, and that my body thought I was still pregnant. Then it occurred to me how odd it was that I only threw up on Monday mornings before leaving for work. I knew then that I was getting a message from my gut, literally, and I'd better listen.

My illness made me realize how unhappy I was with the business, how much I desperately wanted to get rid of it. Yet, every time I began to think about shutting the doors, I couldn't bear the thought of it. It really terrified me. I had worked so hard to build the business, and I excelled at it, especially the creative aspects. When I allowed myself to talk about my fear, to think about the unthinkable, I realized that my real fear in risking a change was the fear of what people in the community would think of me.

Looking back on it, it seems so silly. I was afraid people would think I had failed. And I was tied into being successful, being thought of as a successful woman entrepreneur. I couldn't stand the thought of being the subject of lunchtime gossip around town. So, for another year my pride continued to make me sick; I stayed with the business and I was miserable. It was only when I became miserable enough to stop caring what people thought that I was able to get on with my life. What a painful, valuable lesson.

I shut the agency, helped my employees find new jobs, and sold all the equipment. It was the best decision I ever made. After spending a year consulting, I began a new career in speaking and training, sharing my marketing and creativity expertise with audiences around the country.

Beginning a new career was risky and at times frightening. But by pushing past my fears, my courage muscle began to strengthen.

I still force myself to embrace emotional discomfort regularly. Trying things that frighten me or make me feel insecure or foolish have given me the confidence I need to take on even greater risks. Each small victory gives me the courage to stretch a bit further. I'm doing things now I never dreamed of just a few years ago, because it continually builds my confidence to try.

Nothing stifles creativity like fear of change. Because the rate of change is accelerating, you will need the ability to make change work for you; and that will require taking more risks, more often. The truth is, you can't afford *not* to risk. In fact: **The greatest risk you can take is not to risk.**

If you are standing on a rock that is located at the edge of your ability to jump to shore and you don't try to jump, sure enough the tide will come in and you will drown. If you jump and miss, you'll get wet, but you'll learn to jump and you won't drown. Rarely is the outcome of an imagined fear nearly as bad as we imagine it. Just as there is no way you can remain anchored in a whirlpool without drowning, there is no way to unleash your creativity without learning to push your limits.

We are being deluged by change. You can resist it, be passively swept away by it, or learn to be flexible and enjoy it. By experiencing the creativity that comes from successful risk taking, you will not only conquer your fear of change, you will also learn to embrace all that life has to offer.

EXERCISE

What is a difficult change happening in your life right now—or one that you anticipate? Make a list of every possible benefit that can result from it. List as many positive things as you can, no matter how silly or absurd. Don't stop until you've exhausted every possibility. Reframing the change and focusing on the positive outcomes will help you accept it. From acceptance you can move more comfortably into taking the risks necessary to use the change to best advantage.

The power of changing your attitude to embrace change cannot be overstated. When you change your attitude, seemingly insurmountable obstacles can be mastered and you begin to take charge of your life.

EXERCISE

What is one risk you have been considering taking? What are you afraid will happen if you take this risk? Make a list of the fears that keep you from taking it. List everything you can possibly think of. Put the list away for a day. Take it out and look it over again, evaluating how realistic these fears are. A few of your fears may seem silly now that you see them in writing. Check those off the list. Consider how a change in attitude changes the items on your fear list.

One secret to mastering the art of risk taking is to take on smaller challenges first before you attempt a major change. Make it the smallest risk you can take and still feel that you have been challenged. From success with small risks comes confidence. The best strategy is to break things into small increments and conquer your fear a little at a time.

Salli says:

> Even though I practically grew up in the water, I hadn't been swimming in a long time and was hesitant to go diving with my husband on a recent trip to Mexico.
>
> My husband, a certified scuba diver, helped me conquer my fear by inviting me to swim next to him with a mask on. After a few hours I started feeling comfortable in the water, and as Michael began oohing and aahing over the fabulous fish, I couldn't resist using my snorkel. By the end of our trip, you couldn't get me out of the water, and now one of my life goals is to learn to scuba dive.

Start Small

There are people who enjoy pushing their physical limits, such as rock climbers, bungee jumpers, surfers, and white-water rafters, but most of us are reluctant to take these kinds of risks. Taking small physical risks, however, not only increases your confidence, it adds greatly to your enjoyment of life. Michael Eschenbach, who once flew a glider at 17,160 feet in the mountains just west of Lake Titicaca, Peru, recalls laying the groundwork for taking small physical risks that eventually led to large-scale physical risks. Each successful challenge allowed Michael's confidence to increase, not only in physical sports, but in all areas of his life.

I learned to hang glide on a hundred-foot-tall sand dune in a small town north of San Francisco. I was totally thrilled by the flights, and the risk was small. If you crashed, you only plowed into the sand; the worst outcome was filling every orifice with sand. As I flew more and more, I increased the challenge a little at a time. Eventually I took on the job as a hang gliding instructor, and began flying in other sites around the Bay Area.

A few years later, my brother and I bought a VW pickup truck and took a seven-month driving trip to South America. We took a hang glider with us to fly along the way. We used to flip a coin to decide who would fly and who would film. My first flight came in an area called the Barrancos, just north of Guadalajara, Mexico. The takeoff was in the middle of a maguey cactus field, and once airborne I had to clear a wall of trees, maybe thirty-five feet tall. As I passed over the trees, the ground dropped away, and I was a thousand feet above the ground (about eight hundred feet higher than I'd ever been) and heading down the valley. The flight probably lasted five minutes, but I used every skill I had learned from each of my previous risks to control my speed, manage the variable gusty winds, judge my altitude, and select the landing site. Although I was very scared, I was confident that if I kept my cool, I would do well. Those flights helped me achieve self-confidence and allowed me to take risks in other areas of my life.

For instance, when I started my construction business, I invested quite a bit of money and time into a business that requires long hours and hard work, but offers few guarantees. In fact, most contractors are just carpenters who feel that they would like to work for themselves, as was my case. I really had very little business experience, but I felt confident that if I started with small projects, ones I felt I had a good chance of completing well, I would learn as I went and would succeed. As my business grew, I increased the size and complexity of the projects. I took all of the profits and reinvested them into the business. Each time a client said, "What a beautiful job, thank you for creating it," I felt that the risk had been worthwhile. There were times I underbid a job, but I learned what my mistakes had been and tried not to repeat them. It has been a constant challenge, but I am still taking on larger and more complex jobs and still thoroughly enjoying it.

You ain't living if you ain't breathing hard!

—MAC EAKIN

EXERCISE

Fantasy time! What would you do if you knew it was impossible to fail? Think big! What steps would you have to take to get started? Are you willing to take the first step?

Don't be afraid to go out on a limb—that's where all the fruit is!

—ANONYMOUS

Don't Call It Failure—Call It Research

In addition to fearing what others think, we must also battle the cultural bias against risk. The creative process is a risk process, involving both mistakes and successes.

You learn very early that it's not okay to make mistakes; that right answers are good and incorrect answers are bad. You've learned to keep your mistakes to a minimum by resisting change and avoiding risk. Think about it: In school, if you get the answers right over 90% of the time you receive an A. If you get the right answer over 80% of the time you receive a B; if you get the right answer over 70% of the time you get a C;

and you'll get a D if you get the right answer over 65% of the time. Our schools don't reward coming up with *many* right answers or creative approaches, they reward only *one* right answer. No wonder we're afraid to make mistakes, to break out of our ruts.

Anytime you try something new, you risk failure. Unfortunately, this stops many people from enjoying valuable learning and living experiences. The problem is, most people consider success and failure as opposites, not products of the same process. Prior to the industrial revolution, the words *success* meant journey or progress toward a goal. It was not a destination. When you see your life more as a journey than a series of successes and failures, when you remove the judgment from an event, you free yourself to move ahead without fear. An experience or event only becomes a failure if *you* decide it is a failure. Padi and Salli's motto is: "Don't call it failure, call it research!"

Kate Bishop, who designs clothing from silk, has learned to relish the "research."

It seems to me that everything I've ever done, all the mistakes that I've ever made, have turned out well in the end. When I design a garment that has a really clever detail that gets everybody's attention, you can almost count on the fact that the detail was put on to hide a mistake I'd made. And then it becomes the focal point of the garment and the interesting thing about it.

I've seen my whole life as just making a lot of mistakes and correcting them. As long as you can stick with it . . . If you aren't afraid of your mistakes and just look at them and say, "Oh, what an interesting opportunity; I wonder why I did that—I can't wait to find out!"—You just know that it will turn into something. It doesn't even bother me at all when I make mistakes. I used to have tantrums and cry and throw things. I can't say that it makes me happy, but I have confidence that it's going to turn into something that's better than it would have been if I hadn't made the mistake.

Beware Your Inner Censor

It's precisely her self-forgiving and positive attitude that allows Kate to create such beautiful designs. You, too, can manifest your creativity more fully if you learn to stop censoring yourself and beating yourself up for not being perfect.

> **I** have always grown from my problems and challenges; from the things that don't work out—that's when I've really learned.
>
> —CAROL BURNETT

For some, the very thought of even trying to do something new is too risky. In one of our workshops, participants made a list of everything they wanted to do for the rest of their lives; a life wish list. People listed what they wanted to be, do, and have that was really important to them. Then each person selected one wish and wrote down all the reasons they didn't think they could have it, as a way to get in touch with their inner censor, their voice of judgment.

One man wrote that he wanted to be a filmmaker. His reasons for not pursuing that goal included the following:

"I'm not smart enough."
"I don't have the education."
"I don't have enough talent."

After several minutes, participants were asked what they noticed about their inner censor lists. "It's awfully silly," the would-be filmmaker said, blushing. "I don't know if I'm smart enough or if I have enough talent to be a filmmaker. I haven't even tried yet."

Of course he didn't know if he had any talent. He had never picked up a video camera! Of course he didn't have the education. He had never taken a film class! But what he hadn't realized was that it doesn't take any talent or education to take that first step—to begin. Yet he hadn't begun because he had already given up, without even minimal effort. He had done *absolutely* nothing to move even an inch closer to his dream. All he had done was fill himself with negative messages that stood in the way of his ever trying.

How easily we sabotage ourselves with our negative internal monologue! How easily we are willing to relinquish our power to our frightened inner censor and give up our brightest dreams and hopes without even trying! Few people regret taking risks; many people regret risks they never pursued.

Jean Ruwe, a grandmother of eleven, was not willing to relinquish power to her frightened inner censor.

> I was pressured and persuaded by a number of the players in our dulcimer society to go out and play. It took all the nerve I had, plus not being able to eat beforehand. I was scared to death the first time I did it. . . . After that it came easy because I really loved the instrument. I learned to love performing. I met so many wonderful people who would share their life stories with me, and I found I was very good at talking with people who were so interested in the history of the dulcimer itself. My passion overcame my fear.
>
> It's helped me. I find that now it's so much easier to express myself. I can talk to anyone and not be nervous about it, and I feel I've been even more rewarded than the people I've come into contact with—because of growing myself, plus the fact that I can bring joy and happiness to many people. I've made so many more new friends, really good friends. From taking the risk came much happiness. Not that I wasn't happy before—but it was a different type of happiness.
>
> My husband and I have been married fifty years, and he told me recently, "I can't believe how performing has changed your life!"

EXERCISE

◆ What have you always wanted to do but never tried? Is it time to move this wish into your 10% category?

◆ What is one creative risk you are currently considering?

◆ Why is it important for you to take this risk?

- What are your greatest fears about taking this risk? (Take out the list from the previous exercise and really give it an objective look.)
- What steps can you take to make the risk feel safer to you?
- What would be the worst possible outcome if things didn't work out as planned? What if you "failed"?
- What would your options be then? How would you deal with it?
- If you take this risk, and things work out the way you want, what will be the outcome? Close your eyes and imagine in great detail how your life would be different, how good you would feel about yourself and your accomplishment.

There is nothing of which we are more ashamed than of not being ourselves. And there is nothing which brings us greater joy and happiness than to think, feel, and to say what is ours.

—ERICH FROMM

Salli writes:

The summer I was ten, learning to dive off the high dive became the challenging activity among my friends. The idea of jumping, let alone diving, from that height was terrifying to me, and for several days I invented excuses why I couldn't go swimming. But the desire to be with my friends was too strong; I had to do it. One by one as my friends began to perfect their dives, I began the slow process of conquering my fear of heights.

Day after day I would muster up my courage and climb up the ladder, only to remain frozen with fear at the top. Humiliated, I would then take the long climb back down the ladder. One day the person in back of me, anxious for their turn, refused to let me climb down.

"Don't be such a baby," she taunted, "just jump." And so I did. I wasn't knocked unconscious. I didn't land on the bottom like a rock never again to rise to the surface. In fact nothing bad happened at all. It was just an incredible amount of fun. I couldn't wait to run back up the ladder to try again. Now, when I climbed to the top I didn't have to face the humiliation of climbing back down; now I had a choice, jump or take another risk and dive. It took me an entire summer, and I never became a really good diver, but eventually I did dive off that high board."

The only way to become more comfortable with risk is by risking. Here are some pointers to keep in mind when considering a risk:

- What is your motivation for taking the risk? Make sure it is for yourself, not something you are doing to please someone else. When you risk from the heart, and you feel in your gut that it is right for you, then it is a risk worth taking.
- Make a list of steps necessary to minimize the risk and make you feel safer about it. This could include getting professional advice, calling a group of friends together for emotional support (not advice!), or starting smaller (i.e., turning an avocation into a vocation gradually—step by step).
- Talk with others who are successful risk takers. People who risk well or who took similar risks to the one you are contemplating can act as role models.
- Don't expect a lot of people to share your level of excitement about the risk. Most people don't like to risk change themselves and are uncomfortable around people who are willing to change.
- Most people with ideas that are unique and creative don't get a lot of initial support. There's always someone there to rain on their parade and tell them all the reasons an idea won't work. For example, Harry M. Warner, the president of Warner Brothers, when presented with the radical concept of talking movies in 1927, exclaimed, "Who the hell wants to hear actors talk?"
- "The greatest regret of the terminally ill is 'I made a living but I never really lived,' " says Dr. Elisabeth Kübler-Ross. Remember that the more risks you take, the richer your life will be.

Risking is fundamental to living your life out loud. Break the risk into small parts, and don't move on until you have conquered each part. The secret is to trust in yourself and take one step at a time.

If I am not for myself, who will be for me? If I am not for others, what am I? And if not now, when?
—RABBI HILLEL

We all have our fears and challenges, but as the following American Indian tale teaches, by taking the necessary risks to confront those fears, we enrich our lives and truly become heroes.

THE FLYING HEAD

Long ago, dark spirits and evil monsters terrorized humans. They hid in deep caverns when the sun shone, but on dark, rainy nights they came out of their dens to cause death and destruction. The most frightening creature of all was the horrible Flying Head. It was five times as tall as the tallest man, yet it was only a huge, snarling head without a body. Its eyes were yellow and glowed in the dark like a cat. Two huge bird wings grew from either side of its cheeks, and it could soar around the sky or dive down like a great hawk. No weapon could pierce its leathery, hairy skin. Instead of teeth, the Flying Head had a mouth full of huge, razor-sharp fangs that it used to grab and devour its prey. Every living creature, man and animal, was prey to this monster.

One dark, stormy night, someone in a village spotted the Flying Head darting among the treetops of the forest and told his people to flee. Everyone ran away to hide, except a young woman with a baby, who stayed alone in the longhouse. She had decided not to run away because she thought, someone has to make a stand against this monster. Someone has to risk trying to rid our village of this vile creature. It might as well be me.

So she built a huge fire in the hearth of the longhouse and threw in many large stones, which began to glow red-hot in the dancing flames. She watched the fire and she waited, until suddenly, the Flying Head appeared in the doorway. She pretended not to see its huge, grinning face, its glistening fangs. Instead, she made believe she was eating some of the red-hot stones, picking them up with a big spoon and seeming to put them in her mouth. Smacking her lips, she remarked about the wonderful meal: "Such a great feast! What tender, juicy meat. No one has ever tasted such wonderful food."

When the Flying Head heard her words, its hunger became uncontrollable, and it thrust itself into the lodge, opened its horrible mouth as wide as it could, and seized the whole heap of red, hissing rocks. The moment it swallowed the fiery feast, the monster let out a mournful, ear-piercing cry. It began to flap its huge wings, and it fled screaming out of the longhouse, through the village, over the mountains, forests, and rivers. It screamed so loud and long that the stars shook in the sky, leaves fell off the trees, and the earth below trembled. At last, the screams faded until they could no longer be heard, and people everywhere could take their hands away from their ears. Since that day, the Flying Head was never seen again, and people were no longer afraid of dark, rainy nights.

TO RISK

To laugh is to risk appearing the fool.
To weep is to risk appearing sentimental.
To reach out to another is to risk involvement.
To express feelings is to risk exposing your true self.
To place ideas and dreams before a crowd is to risk their loss.
To love is to risk being loved in return.
To live is to risk dying.
To hope is to risk despair.
To try is to risk failure.
But risks must be taken because the greatest hazard in life is to risk nothing.
The person who asks nothing, does nothing, has nothing, and is nothing.
They may avoid suffering and sorrow, but they
Cannot learn, feel, change, grow, love, live.
Chained by their attitudes, they are a slave.
They have forfeited their freedom.
Only a person who risks is free.

—ANONYMOUS

◆

NURTURING YOUR CREATIVITY

> Cherish forever what makes you
> unique, 'cuz you're really a yawn if
> it goes.
> —BETTE MIDLER

For anything to grow, blossom, or flourish, it must be nurtured. So it is with your creativity. When you treat yourself as the most important person in your life, you can nurture yourself with the same passion with which you nurture anything or anyone you love. The truth is that the more you love and nurture *yourself*, the better you will be able to love and nurture others. When you give yourself permission to develop and express your creativity, you will discover the deep joy that comes from living your life out loud. As Lucille Ball, a woman who truly lived her life out loud, said, "Love yourself first, and everything else falls into line. You really have to love yourself to get anything done in this world."

Nurturing yourself involves letting go of some assumptions about the "shoulds" and "ought tos," and leaping head-on into the "why-nots" and "so-whats." It means being willing to be a beginner again, a learner, an experimenter, no matter your age or what your life has been about up until this *very moment*. It means adopting the philosophy of the ancient Jewish saying: "*Today* is the first day of the rest of your life."

Creativity is about expanding your repertoire. It's about loosening the belt of inhibitions and starting to play again. It's about reconnecting with nature, listening to your inner voice, paying attention to the information and images you create when you sleep, and using the power of your creative mind to program future successes.

As Henry James noted in *The Ambassadors,* "Live all you can; it's a mistake not to. It doesn't so much matter what you do in particular, so long as you have your life. If you haven't had that, what have you had?"

5

The Power of Play

To play is to yield oneself to a kind of magic.
—HUGO RAHNER

Play is not just for children. To regain a sense of joy in our lives, we all need to play. Play not only makes us joyful, it releases our creative juices. As adults, we tend to think of play as frivolous, unproductive activity, "just for kids." And that attitude gets in the way of living our lives out loud.

Ironically, too many people wait until they are nearly dead to discover play and their buried longing for creative expression. The world-renowned authority on death and dying, Dr. Elisabeth Kübler-Ross, has documented countless cases of terminally ill patients finding their creative spirit shortly before they die. In her book *To Live Until We Say Goodbye,* she explains:

> These patients often become poets; they become creative
> beyond any expectations, far beyond what their educational backgrounds prepared them for. . . . The reason for
> all this emerging creativity . . . is the fact that we all have
> many hidden gifts within our own being, and they are all

too frequently drowned in the negative and materialistic struggles on which we spend so much of our precious energy. Once we are able to get rid of our fears, once we have the courage to change from negative rebellion to positive nonconformist, once we have the faith in our own abilities to rise above fear, shame, guilt, and negativity—we emerge as much more creative and much freer souls.

How tragic that for many of us the joy of playful creation comes at the end of life or not at all. We let our fears, shame, and self-consciousness get in the way of our creative potential.

If you want to be joyful, you've got to find ways to express your creative genius—even if you step on your dancing partners' toes, even if you belly flop, even if you end up with more paint on you than on the canvas. You've got to risk singing flat notes, shooting bad films, painting muddy paintings, composing clumsy poems, writing predictable short stories, delivering boring speeches. You've got to risk being an awkward beginner again. Play is *so* important because it lets you be a beginner and experiment with new ways of creating in a nonthreatening way. After all, you're just playing!

Now is the time to indulge yourself and stop worrying about not being good enough, not having enough time, not knowing enough. Now is the time to start unleashing the playful, creative part of yourself that's been ignored and denied for too long. You only have one life, so why not make it as wonderful, playful, joyful, and delicious as it can be?

When you begin expressing yourself in new ways, you strengthen all of your creative abilities. This kind of creative cross-training is not only healthy for your brain, it enriches all of your life as well. Creative play is one of the most nurturing things you can do for yourself and the people around you.

Artist and psychotherapist Sara Alexander says that playful people can be healing and joyful for others to be around. "I had a butcher. When I found out he was retiring, I cried. This man was my *butcher.* He cut meat, but he was so in the moment and so playful, so joyous, you could get completely high waiting for your hamburger! Playful people bring magic and surprise into their lives and others' lives. A good day or good piece of art, or good conversation or good dance choreography has magic and surprise in it.

It takes seventeen muscles to smile and forty-three to frown.

Write Yourself a Play Prescription Today

"When you have a playful attitude, everything seems to go a lot better," says Michael Eschenbach, a general building contractor. "All day long I interact with subcontractors, employees, clients, and suppliers, and I sing and dance with them every chance I get. I try to lighten up every situation. It makes me a lot happier, and people respond by being more playful in return. Even when I'm alone, I'll turn up the radio in the cabinet shop, grab a screwdriver, and pretend it's a microphone!

Unlike Michael, as most people mature, they squelch their fun, playful, and humorous sides. In our creativity workshops, we ask participants to think of the most outrageous thing they ever did or said. It always amazes us to hear that the vast majority of people haven't done or said anything outrageous since they were in their teens or twenties. And most of the participants are in their thirties and older. Perhaps if we asked the question, "Are we having fun yet?" most people would have to answer, "Not anymore."

Play is an attitude as much as anything. One of the things that drew us together to create this book is that we love mixing work and play. We found many opportunities to be playful throughout the book-writing process. Once Salli brought sparkly blue and red starred crowns for her and Padi to wear while they worked; and Padi has been known to pull out cheerleading pom-poms to celebrate progress made. Instilling a sense of fun into the often laborious and challenging task of writing a book made the difficult moments lighter and the good times great.

Play is contagious, like laughter.

It always seems to me that so few people live—they just seem to exist, and I don't see any reason why we shouldn't LIVE always, till we die physically. Why do we do it all in our teens and twenties?

—GEORGIA O'KEEFFE

In our experience, the most creative people have retained the ability to play, and they infuse their work with playfulness. But even beside their work, highly creative people carve time out for *just* play. They make it a priority. We were curious about why playfulness is a prerequisite for creativity, and so we went in search of a play expert.

As you would expect, interviewing the first professional playologist in the world was a zany, wonderful experience. Ellie Katz, herself the epitome of living your life out loud, believes that play is a priority—fundamental to life and survival. She feels that relearning how to play not only increases your creativity, imagination, and intuition, it also brings more joy into your life.

"Play is one of the highest spiritual forms of being. When we're in that state, we get lost in ourselves, which allows the mind to receive the message of the spirit," Dr. Katz observes. She notes that because the world has lost its ability to play, we are experiencing greater loneliness, depression, health problems, communication breakdowns, and the loss of creativity.

Armed with bubble blowers, magic wands, and marshmallows (for throwing at people, of course), she has taught and lectured throughout the United States for nearly two decades in her one-woman crusade to get the world to lighten up and start playing more. Ellie Katz has been described as a walking Mardi Gras because of her colorful, wild clothing and penchant for surrounding herself with whimsical toys and props. Her house is filled with magic wands for "wishing anything you want." When you enter her house, you have instant permission to play, so you do.

Her students have included corporate managers, doctors, psychologists, nurses, and teachers who want to learn playology, which Dr. Katz defines as "relearning the creation of joy." She notes that people in our culture stop spontaneous play by age seven or eight. Then they learn games that have rules. And, she says, "Rules change things: They teach us to forget how to relax, create, and enjoy play. In spontaneous play, nobody cares who wins or loses, so everybody wins," she says.

As we get older, we feel guiltier about playing because our

culture does not support play as a way of learning. Learning is serious business, play is for toddlers. Our culture is so results-oriented, and a lot of play has no immediately discernible end product to show for the time spent. As a result, Dr. Katz believes that we have lost our ability to create and innovate because we haven't sharpened the necessary tools—our play tools. Play is a process that must be constantly polished and practiced if we are to be our most joyful.

Surrounding yourself with reminders of play is one way to keep play in your 10% category. Dr. Katz is a formidable role model in this regard, as her beach house in southern California resembles a giant playground. There's a sign on the front door that says "Take off your shoes and enjoy your feet." Next to the door, floor-to-ceiling shelves overflow with her eclectic collection of shoes, boots, and spangled heels in outrageous hues. Another sign in her front window announces, "Warning: These premises patrolled by rabbits." Inside there are pillows, colorful toys, a giant cargo net, cherub clocks, art, feathers, more signs, and a never-ending supply of magical toys. It is almost impossible *not* to feel playful when surrounded by so much color, fun, and humor.

Padi has a small room filled with props that she uses in her workshops and training programs. A four-foot stuffed orange rayon carrot, a mask of a sheep's head, mental floss (a magic trick that makes it look like you're flossing between your ears), and sticks of satin dynamite are among the bizarre and fun items Padi has collected. She enjoys taking them out to add some pizzazz to a family gathering or bringing them to a client's office just to elicit smiles.

Salli's house is filled with wands, teddy bears, fortune cards, musical instruments, and bathtub toys. When people drop by, they are in the habit of going to her play table and choosing an "angel card" that gives them their special message for the day. All the cards are positive with words like openness, joy, playfulness clarity, balance, freedom, and creativity.

EXERCISE

Buy or make something "childish" that makes you feel good even if it's supposedly for kids. Leave it around the house. Notice how people will pick it up with a happy grin and have some fun with it. Most people are delighted to have any excuse to play a little. The more you play, the more other people will feel it's okay to play. We are all kids at heart, and encouraging playfulness is one of the best gifts we can give one another. Bubble blowers, stuffed animals, yo-yos, Nerf darts, and finger paints are some suggestions.

Crayons and big sheets of paper are great for bringing back happy memories that to most of us represent the most playful and creative time in our lives. A neighborhood restaurant that Salli and her husband love going to provides little buckets of crayons and covers the table with a big sheet of paper to encourage kids of all ages to express themselves in between courses. Suggest this idea to a local restaurant or really live boldly and bring out those crayons and some big sheets of paper and go to it at your own kitchen table.

Turning on More of You

Dr. Katz sees play as the discovery of the self through exploration and imagination. "What turns me on the most is turning on more of me," she says laughing. Through play, she believes, we can discover parts of ourselves we didn't know we possessed. "Playology is about waking up our senses, infusing our organs of seeing, hearing, smelling, touching, tasting—and the higher cognitive senses as well, with the spirit of play. Play ignites creativity and spontaneity. Playing together leads to trust and cooperation."

EXERCISE

Rediscovering childhood pleasures can help uncover forgotten creative play that was once meaningful to you. Make a list of favorite things you loved to do as a child. Did you tap-dance, paint, play the drums, collect insects, build models? After you've listed everything you can think of, go down the list slowly, and when you come to each word, close your eyes and visualize yourself involved in the activity. Try to recreate in your mind the feelings you had while pursuing this favorite form of play.

After you've gone through the entire list, review it again. Are there any activities you would enjoy again now? How can you use the information about past pleasures to create play opportunities in your life now? What clues can you find about what you enjoyed then and what may bring you pleasure now?

Now make a second list. List all the things you wanted to do as a child but were *unable* to do; i.e., what did you want to learn but never had the opportunity? Were you told you were tone-deaf and prohibited from learning to play an instrument or singing in the chorus? (Padi was!) Were you told you couldn't even draw a stick figure? (Salli was!) Were you not allowed to have a drum set because the neighbors in the apartment next door would scream? Are there things you always wanted to do but couldn't? Think about what you would enjoy *now*. It's never too late to learn!

Many participants in our creativity workshops have looked back into their childhood at unfulfilled creative needs and have begun to heal those old wounds and fill those longings.

A forty-six-year-old executive who participated in our training said, "Since I was in sixth grade, I have always wanted to play the guitar. But my family couldn't afford lessons, or a guitar. I always regretted never learning to play, and as I grew up I made excuses for not taking lessons. After the workshop, I decided to take up the guitar, and I've made the time. I'm taking guitar classes with my daughter, and we're learning together. I'm loving it, and we're having a great time!"

Take a Play Risk Today

At a park a few years ago, Padi's three-year-old son pleaded with her to roll down a hill with him. "Oh, no, Mommy can't do that," she explained. When he asked why, she couldn't think of an intelligent answer, so off they rolled. Sweat, grass stains, giggles, and rosy cheeks later, she said it was one of the sweetest times they spent together and remains one of her fondest memories.

We have to stop worrying about what other people think. Most people don't really care anyway, and why waste all that time and energy thinking and worrying when we could be playing instead? So many of us agonize over what others will think when *they're* too busy worrying about what we think of them! If you think back over the best times you've had in your life, you'll probably realize that they occurred when you were more playful, wilder, and more spontaneous than usual. Some of our most playful moments become our most cherished memories, and they come as a result of our willingness to risk being playful.

"A big part of being playful to me is being spontaneous," says Faith Morgan, CEO of Computer Integrated Building Systems.

> One of my happiest memories is when I was working at summer camp teaching kids horseback riding. One night after the kids were all asleep, I got one of the horses out and rode nude in the moonlight. Part of the fun was doing something taboo and part of it was the sense of freedom. I could feel the horse in a way I never could before. It was life itself. It was exhilarating!

Visual artist Carole Rae loves to tell the story of how she and some friends made a Zen priests' bachelor party really special. Carole, who is one of the most creative and playful women we know, conceived the idea of becoming a human hors d'oeuvre. She had always thought it would be wonderful to lay on a table covered in delicious food, and this was her chance.

The day of the party, four women friends bathed her and then rubbed a special cream cheese and sour cream concoction all over her body so the food would stick. She was laid out on the serving table and her head covered with a fern plant for camouflage. Then they stuck all the hors d'oeuvres to her body. A slab of baked salmon was placed down the middle of her chest, sliced meats and cheeses lay across her arms like sleeves, and a turquoise alabaster bowl filled with onion dip sat atop her pubic bone. She was elaborately garnished with fresh parsley, bright red cherry tomatoes, and peppery orange nasturtium blossoms.

The guests arrived, and everyone began sampling hors d'oeuvres and talking gaily. The Zen priests and their friends, the bride and her entourage were all there feasting and visiting. Carole was sure she would be discovered in several minutes, but everyone kept right on nibbling and chatting; totally unaware of the human centerpiece beginning to shiver under all that chilled food. Carole kept as still as she could, though she was getting colder by the minute.

After about an hour had passed, someone cut into the fragrant pink salmon on her chest just as Carole took a breath. The guest stepped backward and asked, "Is this thing plugged in?" At that point, Carole, nearly frozen by now, started laughing. The guests began to crowd around the table, eating faster to reveal the human hors d'oeuvre they had not previously noticed. People were amazed, delighted, amused. A few began licking the cream cheese off her arms and legs.

Finally, Carole announced that she was too cold and just stood up right in the middle of the table. All the parsley, cheeses, cherry tomatoes, meats, and the rest of the poached salmon slid or dropped off her body to the applause of the guests!

If play doesn't come naturally to you, then plan it into your daily schedule, even if it's only a ten-minute mini play break. We guarantee that this will become one of your best-loved habits.

EXERCISE

Make a play day with yourself. Go to a toy store and look around for a while. Treat yourself to a game, a kazoo, anything that catches your eye. Go play with it! Keep it around the house where you can enjoy it and remind yourself to lighten up and play.

TEN MINI PLAY BREAKS THAT TAKE TEN MINUTES OR LESS

- ✦ Keep humorous books of cartoons or short essays on hand at work and at home. Smile emergencies can occur at any time, and the shortest distance between two moods (angst and joy) is humor.
- ✦ Take off your shoes, wiggle your toes, and give yourself a foot massage.
- ✦ Prepare your favorite childhood delicacy, and *don't* clean up as you go. Spaghetti with ketchup, bananas and peanut butter, Rice Crispy squares, a mayonnaise and onion sandwich; anything goes.
- ✦ Put on some relaxing music, loosen your clothing, close your eyes, and have a bona fide daydream.
- ✦ Crossword puzzles, brain teasers, and logic problems challenge the mind and are fun to do. There are many excellent paperbacks available to keep around for quick play breaks.
- ✦ Sketch something in your immediate surroundings. Really look at it closely and notice all the details you've never seen before.
- ✦ Put on some upbeat rhythmic music, and turn your kitchen into an instant percussion section. Play the spoons, beat on some pans, put some dried beans in a pot and shake it up!
- ✦ Write a poem or silly limerick. Remember, you don't have to show it to anyone, so let loose! The point is to have fun.
- ✦ Change your outfit to change your attitude. Put on the wildest clothing combo you can and spend the day that way.
- ✦ Get wet. Take a walk in the rain. No umbrellas allowed.

We do not stop playing because we grow old; we grow old because we stop playing.

—ANONYMOUS

Storyteller and teacher Ruth Stotter puts play on her "to do" list as an everyday reminder to make sure she leaves time for the things she loves, like hiking or bike riding. This idea was suggested to her by a colleague who encouraged her to create more playtime in her life.

One day Ruth's friend, Andrea, a harpist, invited her to come visit and listen to a new piece of music she was working on. Ruth declined, saying she had a class to prepare for that evening. Unwilling to take no for an answer, the friend queried, "Have I ever asked anything of you?" Ruth realized she hadn't and sheepishly went. An afternoon of music, bike riding, and visiting drifted on, with Ruth mentioning at a few junctures, "I really ought to be going." But her friend insisted she stay "just a bit longer." Finally, Ruth could wait no longer, having barely enough time to shower and change clothes before her class. "You know what?" she says smiling. "It was the best class I ever taught."

> You can discover more about a person in an hour of play than in a year of conversation.
>
> —PLATO

EXERCISE

Make a list of activities you would enjoy and the people you would enjoy playing with. Perhaps taking a class, walking, going dancing, learning a new language, playing cards or a sport. Playing with our friends is a habit we lose too easily in childhood. Scheduling fun time with friends on a regular basis can help you recapture the joys of play. Make play dates with friends you've missed.

Play is one of the greatest incubators, as it often brings about the alpha brain wave state. "Your brain controls how you feel," says Dr. Katz. "It's the biggest playground in the world. What we think and feel creates secretions from the brain, which in turn causes biochemical changes throughout the body. When we laugh and play, our body releases endorphins, the body's natural opiates." Endorphins produce feelings of well-being happiness, and contentment. We only need to give ourselves the gift of play to release them. In the wise words of Ellie Katz: "Take a play break, and make a breakthrough to you!"

CERTIFICATE OF THE RIGHT TO PLAY

(This certificate was given to us by Herman Warsh, play connoisseur at a small get-together of friends one evening. The author is unknown, and if you find out who it is, please give that person a hug from us!)

By this certificate know ye that _____ is a lifetime member in good standing in The Society of Childlike Persons and is hereby and forever entitled to: walk in the rain, jump in mud puddles, collect rainbows, smell flowers, blow bubbles, stop along the way, build sand castles, watch the moon and stars come out, say hello to everyone, go barefoot, go on adventures, sing in the shower, have a merry heart, read children's books, act silly, take bubble baths, get new sneakers, hold hands and hug and kiss, dance, fly kites, laugh and cry for the health of it, wander around, feel scared, feel sad, feel mad, feel happy, give up worry and guilt and shame, stay innocent, say yes, say no, say the magic words, ask lots of questions, ride bicycles, draw and paint, see things differently, fall and get up again, talk with animals, look at the sky, trust the universe, stay up late, climb trees, take naps, do nothing, daydream, play with toys, play under the covers, have pillow fights, learn new stuff, get excited about everything, be a clown, enjoy having a body, listen to music, find out how things work, make up new rules, tell stories, save the world, make friends with the other kids on the block, and do anything else that brings more happiness, celebration, relaxation, communication, health, love, joy, creativity, pleasure, abundance, grace, self-esteem, courage, balance, spontaneity, passion, beauty, peace, and life energy to the above named member and to other humans and beings on this planet. Further, the above named is hereby officially authorized to frequent amusement parks, beaches, meadows, mountaintops, swimming pools, forests, playgrounds, picnic areas, summer camps, birthday parties, circuses, cookie shops, ice cream parlors, theaters, aquariums, zoos, museums, planetariums, toy stores, festivals, and other places where children of all ages come to play, and is encouraged to always remember the motto of The Society of Childlike Persons:

It's never too late to have a happy childhood!

6

Listen to Your Inner Voice

We are so many selves. It's not just the long-ago child within us who needs tenderness and inclusion, but the person we were last year, wanted to be yesterday, tried to become in one job or in one winter, in one love affair or in one house where even now, we can close our eyes and smell the rooms. What brings together these ever-shifting selves of infinite reactions and returnings is this: There is always one true inner voice. Trust it.

—GLORIA STEINEM, *Revolution from Within*

Each of us is born with a unique, essential gift. This gift is a sacred trust that is both our responsibility and our joy to evolve. It is the thread of our existence. This chapter is about getting in touch with your special gift: the one and only unique you!

Connecting with your creative channel unleashes a powerful learning and healing force in your life. As you learn to trust your inner voice, it feels so right, so good, so nurturing. You become whole and fulfilled. You become as you are meant to be. You know what to do.

Let me listen to me and not to them.

—GERTRUDE STEIN

We live in a culture that provides little support for the inner voice, a culture that has all but extinguished the essential spark within each of us.

As children we quickly learn to fit in, to keep our creative treasures to ourselves. The fear of rejection and loss of love is so scary that we learn to hide our inner light, sometimes even from ourselves. Protecting that inner light is a healthy response, but after years of hiding, it's difficult to find our way back.

Most of us have been taught to block our creativity for fear of being labeled strange or different, of not fitting in, as if we are *supposed* to be the same! So strong is the cultural denial of the inner world that many people don't even realize they have one.

You must rediscover the necessary tools if you are to unlock your creativity. The more your inner gifts are revealed, the more joyful you will become. In this chapter you'll discover those tools, powerful concepts along with simple exercises, to help you access the richness of your inner world. Even though you might be the most incredible person inside, if you are unable to let that beautiful being out, it won't do anyone any good.

Paying Attention to Your Inner Voice

I think the one lesson I have learned is that there is no substitute for paying attention.

—DIANE SAWYER

Kat Harrison, president of Botanical Dimensions, is learning to access her inner world and notes that it takes practice and lots of attention:

I try to pay attention to my intuition, my inner voice. In making little choices I try to do the thing that just pops in. I learned from a powerful woman in Peru about paying attention to what her community refers to as the "invisible level." To me, that invisible level represents the little thoughts that come to you unbidden, or when you notice something out of the corner of your eye, or data that you didn't intend to be there, but somehow unexpectedly keeps appearing in little tiny ways that you tend to dismiss. In our society we call it our imagination, which means it's not really valuable, or we think of it as an accident, or, "Hmmm that's interesting, but *this* is my agenda for today."

This woman told me that all the unbidden stuff, all the little tiny fragments of the unexpected, that's what we are supposed to pay attention to. She said to me, "That's the World talking to you."

Intuition is a much more important channel than we acknowledge. Most of us were raised to doubt ourselves and to believe that the only information that counted was of a factual, practical nature. "I feel if we can learn to listen to that little voice coming in that we generally dismiss, then we will find ourselves doing the right thing," Kat observes, "We will learn to be in correct relationship with nature and with each other."

All of us have a longing to express ourselves, to put our inner selves out into the world, to set free our joy and creativity. This is instinctive. When we are not tuned into our inner world, there is an underlying, undefined sense that a key part of ourselves is underground.

Deena Metzger talks about this schism in *Writing for Your Life:* "Each of us has been undermined and diverted from ourselves by a series of small incidents and assaults from various quarters; from these experiences we learned, carefully and painfully, that it was best to go underground."

The need to go underground, this constraint on our true nature and the constant push to conform, exacts a very heavy toll. The denial of our inner voice plays a dominant role in depression, which is epidemic in our culture, a depression that has systematically steamrolled our joy and our creativity.

If you connect with your own mind deep enough, it reverberates for everyone. That's what we call art.
—NATALIE GOLDBERG

Unlock Your Creativity and Throw Away the Key

Audrey von Hawley enrolled in a year-long doll-making class to help unlock her creativity. The project required that everyone in the class make a life-size doll of some aspect of themselves. An incredible amount of introspection and care went into the making of each doll. It was a very powerful and moving experience, and through the process of making her doll, Audrey gained a lot of insight into what was blocking her artistic growth.

When I was little the only emotion I was allowed to express was laughter or happiness. I wasn't allowed any emotional outlet for my anger, sadness, jealousy, or any other negative emotion because it wasn't accepted in my family. So any emotion I felt came out as laughter. I still laugh a lot, even at things that are sad or horrible.

All my life I believed I couldn't express deep emotion, but it turns out I didn't even know how to *feel* deep emotion. I had sealed my pain and grief and anger off with a thick layer of cement. Every time I felt something, I would cover it up with another layer of cement. Just get out my little trowel and cover it up. Yet, deep emotion is where everything juicy comes from. During the doll class it was very scary and painful as I was learning to connect with myself, but it was well worth it. I wrote this poem during the process:

I see the frightening abyss beneath the cement of my fears.
I will not go down, not go down.
I am drowning, drowning. No no no.
Here I am with the demons and dragons of myself.
Down where the anger lives, where the pain lives and waits
    to be felt,
so the passion and creativity can come out.
Go down so you can come up whole with all your parts.

The cement is broken up now. I have experienced the going down and the coming up. At the end of the doll-making process, there was a very powerful show that was open to the public, and most of us wrote a statement to accompany our dolls. This was mine:

I came to Audrey to show her she can manifest something beautiful and awe-inspiring. That she has a gift to share with the world and now she knows she can do it. She can share it and make herself fulfilled and make others feel fully. She does not have to hold back because she now knows that the way to her creative expression is down deep where the pain has lived and the anger has smoldered and the power has been suppressed. She has the key to her own future, knowing that the only barriers were her own limiting beliefs; the beliefs that the gates were closed and locked.

Mirium Redstone, a psychotherapist who works with women in transition, often deals with the results of "gates that are closed and locked." "We start with our essence," she explains:

Our essence has a right to be.

I feel we have the right to be ourselves. In my family that was not allowed. I think it's the same for most of us. We come into the world. Our essence isn't allowed. So we create a defense system that allows us to survive. It's an incredibly creative thing we all do; it's our most creative act, this defense system. And then when we get older, if we are lucky, we can exist with more support, and we can drop that defense system, because it's no longer necessary. For myself, now that survival is not at stake, I have created a simple enough life with people around me who are supportive; I have created space around me for my essence to be.

This planet is about yin and yang; it's about male and female. About pain and joy. It's about dark and light. I use the metaphor of a seed. The essence of a seed is we put it in the ground with its coat of food around it. It's dark, and then if the seed gets nourishment, it sprouts. People are scared to go into the dark. We don't have experience with the dark. Yet, there is a whole world in the dark.

If you do not express your own original ideas, if you do not listen to your own being, you will have betrayed yourself.

—ROLLO MAY

Nurturing the Silence

What grows makes no noise.

—GERMAN PROVERB

The single most important tool to help you pay attention to your inner voice is to learn to be quiet—to nurture the silence so your essence can be heard.

Sometimes going on retreat is the only way you can create the necessary space and quiet to learn the lessons that will help you pay attention to your own wisdom. Delia Moon, psychology student at Pacifica Graduate Institute in Santa Barbara, California, spent ten days in the desert to get in touch with her inner voice. Three weeks after her husband died, she went on a vision quest to the High Desert, her latest in a lifelong series of quests after inner truth and peace.

In her daily journal Delia wrote:

Too often we carry within our wounded hearts, stunted by the trauma of so-called "civilized" life, a resistance to feel and to savor the creative joy that is our human birthright. Deep within the psyche of each sentient being is a safe space that nurtures the germ of self-healing and growth. It is a place of infinite and timeless wisdom and, in the silence of the mountaintop, the dry desert wind, the pounding surf, the thundering or trickling creek, in the peace of the sunlit valley, I have sought and found the regenerative power of this space. An ability to focus and quiet the mind is necessary to create a state from which self-knowledge, self-love, and self-esteem may grow.

What a lovely surprise to discover how unlonely being alone can be.

—ELLEN BURSTYN

In the silence of the desert, also, Kandis Kozolanka learned to savor her creative joy and to experience herself in new ways by assisting in several vision quests. Because of the profound impact of her own experiences, she occasionally acts as a guide so that others can experience the power of "listening to themselves." Kandis states:

> When you go to that underworld place, you are gathering information from your private well. Going out into the desert within a safe container . . . having someone watch over you in a way that lets you know what the dangers are without interfering, allows you to be quiet and listen to your own inner voice so that you will know what you need to do in your life.
>
> Knowing that I have a voice and actually listening to it are really important to me. I'm finding that every time I have an inkling about something or an intuition about something and I ignore it, I get into a lot of trouble. I have paid a really high price for ignoring my own voice. But when I listen, when I pay attention, things work out for me. Instead of seeking validation from somebody else, I'm learning to honor my own inner voice.

Vision quests or any retreat can be extremely healing and liberating for our spirits. The first time fine artist Carole Rae went on a meditation retreat, it wasn't just to find quiet and space; she had developed tendonitis in both arms and was an emotional wreck.

> The tendonitis wasn't only about physical labor. I had rented my house in the city to some artists, and they put all their art supplies in front of the heater. In the night the thermostat came on, and my house was torched. It went up in flames. Through the roof and floor down into the basement. Two weeks after I had single-handedly finished painting the house and making it all beautiful for them to move into, I had to come back and rebuild and repaint.
>
> My husband and I were also building a house in the

country, and I had to commute to the city and rebuild my house all over again. And in the middle of that process the tenants decided to sue me. I was so furious! So I had a lot of emotional trauma along with the physical trauma. A friend said: "Go and sit at the Vipassana for ten days and be quiet and let it all go." I had never done anything like that before. Never in my life had I been quiet without talking for ten days.

During that experience I got so happy. You begin to feel every square inch on your body. You start at the top of your head and you go around and you feel what's happening in your body. It's amazing how much sensation there is in your body and how connected it is with what's happening emotionally. I saw that a lot of the pain that I had was unexpressed anger . . . stuff that I had just shoved because I didn't want to deal with it. You bring what's inside out, and then the pain goes away.

By the time I left there, my arms were fine. I forgave the tenants, who, after all, didn't mean to burn down my house and were just angry at themselves. I forgave somebody that I had hated for twenty years because of some major trauma he and I had gone through. I never really knew how to forgive people. That was an incredible gift. Every year I go back, and I sit for ten days. It's important to me to set aside this time for myself. I do it because I become more joyful, and my wisdom deepens from the experience.

No matter how creative you are, you can be so much more. We humans have so much and use so little. Not only do we use but a tiny portion of our intellectual capacity, we tap into only a small sliver of our potential for joy and creativity. Here are some exercises you can start right now to create the solitude and quiet it takes to chip through your cement blocks as you begin to rediscover your creative genius.

EXERCISE

Spend a day in complete silence, from the time you get up in the morning until you go to sleep. Unplug the phone, so you won't be tempted, and stay home or go someplace where you won't run into people you know or have to talk to anyone. A day of quiet is like a fast for your mind; cleansing, refreshing, and healthy. Quieting yourself will enable you to listen better to your mental chatter and notice if it needs adjusting, as well as opening the gates to letting your creative ideas pour forth.

EXERCISE

Take a breakation: Take yourself away, alone. Sleep somewhere different—a hotel room, a friend's house, under the stars. If you can only escape for a night, that's fine. What we're looking for here is a change of pace, perspective, and scenery. Wake up with nothing on your agenda. Don't relate to anyone else, no phone calls, no drive to the corner store. Make no plans. Follow what your instincts tell you. How does this feel for you? Write a letter to yourself about the experience. Save it and reread it once a month as a reminder to schedule more breakations, more often.

Carole Rae is committed to paying attention to her inner voice. She explains:

No new movements, no courses in becoming, no other directions from anywhere are capable of creating you. Your own deep core structure is your guide, and only you can let it loose, let it build, and let it be. Being yourself is terrifying; there are no rules, there are no rights or wrongs, there is no perfect or imperfect, there is only acceptance of whatever is happening on a real, instinctive, subconscious basis. You are the only guide to your pure and honest self. Probably the only thing that is lacking is your ability and willingness to listen to that deep, quiet self.

In this whirlwind society it can be extremely challenging to create the necessary space to listen to that deep, quiet self Carole talks about. It's very difficult to pay attention when there is so much distraction. Yet the rewards are so great. Victoria Whitehand, teacher and artist, has learned to transform her inner energies and emotions into elegant and whimsical clay figures. She wrote the following poem about the inner voice and the joy of self-expression:

> The sages speak of music
> Heard so deeply
> That it is scarcely heard at all:
> But we are that music,
> While the music lasts
>
> What is the music
> Of the silent spaces within?
> It is joy!
> What is the music
> Of the dancing spheres?
> Vast, luminous reaches of space
> Beyond our sight
> Reverberate with consciousness
> and joy!

Here are some ways to begin to uncover your inner treasures, to rebalance and get in touch with your vital seed that's in the dark waiting to sprout.

- Keep a personal journal. Commit to writing in it at least ten minutes every day. Write about what you are feeling and why.
- Spend time alone every day without distractions.
- Go on a vision quest or spiritual retreat for your next vacation.
- Learn to meditate.
- Discover yoga and its varied breathing techniques for excellent stress reduction and mind-quieting.

The first step in the challenging and exciting process of getting in touch with your inner world is to acknowledge that a significant part of yourself has lain dormant, probably for most of your life. And to realize that everyone has an inner world that has been neglected and untended.

The second step is to understand and accept that you have been conditioned to avoid going within, conditioned to deny your truth.

The third step is to risk going beyond the fear and learn to trust that the risk is worth it. Although the inner territory is uncharted, and sometimes frightening, reconnecting with your inner world is the most rewarding treasure you will ever discover. When you reconnect with your inner world, the treasures unearthed will never tarnish, and with each discovery your personal treasure chest will grow. When you discover the joy of becoming whole, you will greet each day with zest, wondering, what will my life reveal today!

7

Wake Up to Your Dreams

Dreams are the angels of our spirits.
—SARK

Considering that we spend about a third of our lives asleep, it's worth paying attention to what goes on behind closed eyes. We each dream approximately two hours each night, which for most of us will add up to spending six years in the dream state.

Dreaming provides a direct channel to your unconscious, a route into a rich pool of creativity that is yours for the taking. You can use your dreams for direct inspiration, guidance to break through creative blocks, and insights into new ways of looking at your life. Sigmund Freud observed that dreams are the "royal road to the unconscious mind." When you are dreaming, there are no restraints on your creativity. Let's look at how you can tap deep into your dreaming state for new levels of insight and creativity.

Ancient kings had dream interpreters, and contemporary psychologists look to their clients' dreams for clues about their deepest fears and desires. Since antiquity, history has been filled with examples of people who sought the wisdom of their dreams and followed them.

Many great creators trusted their dreams to help them. Novelist Robert Louis Stevenson, for example, dreamed plots for his stories, and if he didn't like the ending, he would ask for another one and go back to sleep until the right one appeared.

Naomi Epel, dream expert and author of *Writers Dreaming,* found that many accomplished writers use the images and feelings in their dreams for inspiration. "Creative people apply their craft to their dreams. Artists tap into their dreams and craft these universal images so that they can communicate the emotions we all share." In her book she tells how William Styron, author of *Sophie's Choice,* woke up one morning recalling remnants of a dream with an image of a woman he had known as a young man. "He knew he had to abandon the book he was working on and tell her story. That morning, he started writing *Sophie's Choice.*

Master of the horror genre Stephen King dreamed the resolution for his best-seller *IT.* "He got stuck, asked his unconscious for help, and dreamed he was in a junkyard at the very point where he was stuck in his book. The resolution to the story came to him in his dream," Naomi explains. Children's poet Jack Prelutsky dreams endings to his poems, which he catches by keeping a notebook beside his bed. Novelist Bharati Mukherjee has dreams in which her characters appear to her and tell her how to change the ending.

Dreams have not only helped writers, but creative performers in many other fields as well. When golfer Jack Nicklaus was in a slump during the early 1970s, he dreamed of a winning new method to grip his club. At his next golf match, he regained his championship stature. In 1983, wind surfer Doug Hunt performed one of the first aerial loops on a sailboard after having practiced the stunt in his dreams.

Elias Howe, inventor of the sewing machine, was struggling with how to complete his invention when the answer came to him in a dream. Actually, it was a nightmare, in which he was captured by cannibals and taken before their king, who said, "I command you on the pain of death to finish this machine." While this was happening, Elias noticed that the savages surrounding the king were holding spears with holes drilled into the tips of them. Ah-ha! This gave him the idea of moving the hole in the machine's needle to the tip, and enabled him to complete his invention.

When Mahatma Gandhi was seeking a nonviolent way to attain independence for India in the 1920s, the idea for his twenty-four-hour general strike appeared to him in a dream.

Many years ago when Conrad Hilton decided to buy the hotel that is now the Chicago Hilton, he submitted a sealed bid for $165,000. The following morning, he awoke from a dream with the amount of $180,000 stuck in his mind, so he went and changed his bid. He won the bidding process, as the second highest bid turned out to be $179,800.

Yes, Virginia, dreams are worth paying attention to!

When you invite the unconscious to take control and speak directly to you, many inspirations are awakened. Dreams, your own personal creative metaphors, can move you from one level of awareness to another. They come out of the dark, instinctual inner world of symbols and pictures and can be significant allies in your life. In Greek, the word *metaphor* means transformer, the crossing over of energy from one level to another. We dream in metaphors that contain rich life-transforming messages. We have only to trust the wisdom of our dream allies.

Those who lose dreaming are lost.

—AUSTRALIAN ABORIGINAL PROVERB

But I Never Dream

Although many people insist they do not dream at all, studies indicate that we all dream each night for short periods, every ninety minutes or so. Researchers have estimated that unless we awaken immediately, however, 95% to 99% of those dreams go unremembered.

We are often unaware of our dreams due to a kind of amnesia caused by a brain chemical that gets cut off in the lighter phase of sleep but is present moments before falling asleep and upon awakening. The trick, then, is to learn to catch our dreams while we are in this receptive state.

According to Native American legend, all dreams float in the evening air and are caught by the dream catcher. Traditionally, a web was woven inside a round hoop and placed above an infant's cradleboard. The grandmother made the dream catcher for the newborn, and it was hung on the baby's cradle to assure good dreams and a quiet baby. The dream catcher was treasured throughout life and embellished with meaningful fetishes and personal treasures to enhance its power. The web of the dream catcher was supposed to filter every dream, letting only the good ones flow through the open circle. Good dreams find their way to the sleeper, and bad dreams remain caught in the web, to be dispersed when struck by the first rays of the morning sun, and never heard from again.

Intrigued by this tradition, Salli made her grandson Miles Dylan a dream catcher out of wool and silk she had spun herself and looks forward to helping him add his own mementos as he grows to manhood.

Working with your dreams is a lifelong process that begins with the decision to listen to them. Our degree of interest in anything, dreams included, usually determines whether we remember or not. Keep a dream journal beside your bed to write down any dreams or fragments upon awakening; this will help trigger your remembering response and make recording easier. Another good way to improve dream recall is to give yourself the suggestion just prior to going to sleep that you want to remember your dreams. Well-known dream researcher Dr. Stanley Krippner recommends that if you draw a blank in the morning, free-associate on the first picture or word that pops into your mind as a way to recreate your dream.

Many cultures take seriously the messages in their dreams. This folktale from Haiti warns and reminds us to honor our dreams.

THE MAN WHO WOULD NOT LISTEN TO HIS DREAM

There were once two friends who were so poor that they decided to leave their village in hopes of finding their fortune elsewhere. Day after day they walked and walked, across sand and stone, until one of the friends could walk no farther. He lay down to rest, while the other continued. He walked a little farther, and at last he lay down to rest under an orange tree.

As he slept he dreamed and in his dream he heard a voice that said, "The princess is ill. You can be the one to cure her if you take a leaf from this orange tree and make a tea with it."

In the morning, the man woke up and broke off a large leaf from the tree. He continued on his way until he came to the next town, where he went to the king's house. There was a sign on the door: "Quiet! The princess is ill."

He knocked on the door, and when the king answered it, he told him that he had come to cure the princess. "Dear sir," said the king, "if the greatest doctors in all of Haiti have not been able to cure her, how will a poor man like you do it?"

The man persisted, and finally the king let him in. He went straight to the princess's room, where for three days and three nights he spoon-fed her orange-leaf tea. After three days, she was cured. The king was so delighted, he gave the man three quarters of his fortune and the princess for his wife. The couple were very happy together. But the man had a good memory and did not forget his friend, so after a time, he traveled over the mountains to the village where he had last seen him. When he finally found him, he was as poor as when they had parted. So, the lucky one gave his friend a sack of gold, after telling him how he had come to marry the princess, how the voice in his dream had visited him beneath the orange tree, how he had cured the princess. Then he wished him well and went home to his wife.

But the friend was jealous and thought, "If he can hear voices in his dreams, so can I." He walked to the hill his friend had described and lay down under the orange tree.

Soon, he was asleep. He began to dream, and a voice came to him and said, "Go away." But the man just rolled over. Again, the voice warned, "Go away." The man would not listen. A third time the voice pleaded, "Go away."

The man would not listen to his own dream. He did not move from under that orange tree. In the morning his body was found, eaten by wild dogs and ferocious demons of the night.

Adapted from *The Magic Orange Tree and Other Haitian Folktales,* stories collected by Diane Wolkstein (Alfred A. Knopf, 1978).

Honoring Your Dreams

Many dreams only take a few minutes of contemplation to decipher, and since you know yourself better than anyone, chances are you can be your own best dream analyst.

Analysis doesn't have to be a major undertaking. "It's not so much about analyzing your dreams," dream expert Naomi Epel explains. "It's about honoring them." Naomi suggests that people take action on their dreams. "If you dream about your grandmother, for example, light a candle for her, or ask yourself what advice she would have for you at this time," she adds. "Ask yourself, what can I do to honor the image in the dream?" Naomi also suggests planting something or writing a letter as a way to honor our dreams.

By honoring our dreams, we can gain deeper insights into our fears, our needs, and our truths. We can not only harvest creative ideas, but creative solutions to some of life's most challenging problems. A friend of ours had been very depressed about a business partnership that was no longer meeting his needs. He could not figure out how to unravel himself from his dilemma, and he struggled with the problem for three years. One night he dreamed he was riding in a beautiful vintage car that had once belonged to him. His partner was driving it because in the dream she now owned it, and deeply regretting that he had sold it to her, our friend offered to buy it back. She happily agreed to sell it to him, and together they discussed the terms of the purchase. When he awoke, he realized he had dreamed the solution to his nagging business problem. He would buy back the partnership that she had originally purchased from him, just as he arranged to buy the car back from her in the dream! He would then be free to find a new buyer to sell his business to, one who shared his goals and was more compatible with his style. Two weeks after his dream, a new buyer had been found and an agreement reached with his partner.

Some dreams are obvious and quite specific. Padi's husband, Reuben, was born with the name Ronald, yet from the time he was a small boy, he never felt that his name fit. He was called Curly as a kid, and then Ron and later Ronald, but none of these names ever felt right for him. When he was in his mid-thirties, he had a dream that he was hiking in the Sierras and met his double coming toward him on the trail. "Who are you?" he asked. "I'm Reuben," his mirror image replied. Reuben was his spiritual Hebrew name, which he had never considered using, but when he had the same dream again the following night, he decided to listen and he changed his name.

A dream which has not been interpreted is like a letter unread.
—Yiddish proverb

Sometimes our conscious mind plays tricks on us, hiding truths that are painful for us to look at. The unconscious wants to protect us and sends us survival messages through our dreams. This happened to Jane, a workshop participant who used to travel half the year for business. A dynamic and self-assured executive, Jane believed she had a solid marriage until she was alerted through a dream. Jane dreamed that she and her husband and best friend went to a slumber party held in a gymnasium. When it was time to go to sleep, Jane couldn't find her husband or her best friend. She felt lonely and worried. As she walked around the gym peering into each sleeping bag, a sense of unease blew through her dream. At last she saw her friend's long blond hair. "Oh, Laura, I'm so relieved to have found you," she said, laughing. Her smile froze, however, as she recognized her own husband's boots at the foot of the bag. She felt that the dream was a warning to stop traveling so much and pay more attention to her marriage, so that's what she did.

Faith Morgan, president of CIB, creators of computer software for builders, once had a very prophetic dream.

Faith told us: "I write my dreams down; I keep a book by my bed, and sometimes I'll wake up in the middle of the night with my dream, and I'll go in the other room and write it down and any thoughts I have about it. I pay attention when they come along. Dreams are invaluable. Because of one of my dreams, my husband and I stopped working with a venture capitalist who then later tried to sue us. In the dream I threw a grenade as far away from our place of business as I could, and it exploded, but it didn't destroy us. I knew that the venture capitalist was the grenade; his image came immediately to mind. I just had to pay attention to my dream, even though we really needed the money. That dream probably saved our company.

Faith had another dream that was also important in the growth of her business.

I was working on this stone building, and then it all started to collapse. In the dream I suddenly noticed the building didn't have any foundation. When I awakened, I realized that like that building our business also didn't have a solid foundation in place yet, and it was important to build it right from the ground up. Our business is growing very fast at the moment, and it's important that we don't just skyrocket over the hill without a solid foundation.

Dreaming permits each and every one of us to be quietly and safely insane every night of our lives.

—WILLIAM DEMENT

Capturing Your Dreams

Delia Moon has been studying her dreams for many years.

I keep paper and pencil near my bed, but when I wake up I tell the dream to myself first. My assumption in doing dream work is that everything in the dream is a part of me. If I dream of you, you are, of course, also you, but you are also a reflection of me. When I retell my dream, I always use the present tense to keep it in the moment. I think about what part of me the dream represents. When I do this I often get in touch with parts of me I'd rather ignore. I keep in mind that the dream reflects just a part of me, and it enables me to feel more forgiving of myself. Sometimes dreams help me to acknowledge the forbidden and then let it go. Dreams widen my view of myself and others, too. I have come to see that we have many layers and possibilities.

Dream Seeding and Lucid Dreaming

Dream seeding, a very potent technique, involves writing down a question you wish to have answered in your dream, and putting it under your pillow before going to sleep. Some people even create a special bedtime ritual by writing the question several times, lighting a candle, and meditating on the question further before drifting off. This is honoring your dream in advance!

If you find it difficult to come up with a simple question for your dream, the practice of writing thoughts about your request, or even doodling the problem to get a graphic interpretation of it, can be helpful in clarifying and developing your question. Trying to describe the problem in a few different ways—with words or pictures—can further help you crystallize the question. Rather than focusing the question negatively on what isn't working ask yourself: "What do I want to create or change?" By concentrating on the result you want to achieve rather than the challenge, you free yourself to consider more possibilities and solutions. Once the question is developed, ask yourself for a dream about it.

EXERCISE

Dream seed tonight. Think about an area in your life in which you could use some insight, advice, or guidance. Write your question on a piece of paper, place it under your pillow, and as you drift off to sleep, think about your question. Tell yourself three times that you will remember your dream upon awakening. You may need to do this for a few nights in a row to receive a dream you remember. Just make sure to keep pencil and paper by your bed so you can jot down the dream as you awaken.

Delia Moon explains her approach:

If I feel I need a dream to teach me, I clear my mind before going to bed and then ask for a dream. Sometimes it works and sometimes it doesn't. Sometimes the dream seems to have nothing to do with what I am working on. But I have discovered that dreams are like poetry; they do not always provide clear guidelines but only hints and oblique references. If the dream message is unclear, I use a technique I learned in a dream group. I explore the dream by describing the objects and people as if they were me. For instance, I may have a dream, and there is a chair in it. Perhaps it is ornate and a bit rickety. I will consider how this applies to me. Since I am neither old nor rickety, I will think about what might be making me feel shaky. Dreams help me deal with the emotional, the practical, and the theoretical.

Lucid dreaming allows some people to become the choreographers of their own dreams. Lucid dreaming is when you become aware of the fact that you're dreaming *while* you are dreaming and can direct the action in the dream. This takes a lot of practice, but it can be an interesting journey between the conscious and unconscious minds. It takes dream seeding one step further and can yield more creative fuel for adventurous dreamers.

When a dream is finished, wake up but try not to open your eyes right away, as visual stimulation may distract you. Go over the dream in your mind before writing it down. Dreams fade quickly, and writing them down or tape recording them assures that you will capture the information.

Dream Groups

Dream groups are another good method to unlock the mysteries of your mind and stimulate latent creative problem-solving abilities. In the early seventies, Salli helped lead an ongoing dream class at a local university. Once a week, students came together to share their dreams in a safe, supportive, and comfortable setting free from any distraction. Participants were encouraged to ask questions to help each other remember as much detail as possible and to comment on patterns and similarities from other dreams. Instead of interpretation, each person's dreams were nurtured by the group. Preparing for the class got the students in the habit of recording their dreams each morning, and by the end of the semester, dream sharing had become an important ritual in each of the participant's lives.

We don't interpret a dream, we bring it back to life.
—FRITZ PERLS

Kat Harrison is an ethnobotanist and president of Botanical Dimensions, an organization that collects living plants and surviving plant lore from cultures practicing folk medicine in the tropics. She helps maintain extensive botanical gardens in Hawaii and Peru and participated in a dream group when she last visited Peru.

I had dreams using plants on my last trip there that were just amazing. They really woke me up to the power of dreams and sharing them in a group. To the people in Peru, each species of plant has a particular character, a particular spirit, a story, a song, an attitude. There are even jealous plants and generous plants, for instance. The people put a few leaves of a plant under their pillow at night to draw information from it in their sleep, and then they ask each other their dreams in the morning. As a group they consider, "What did that plant tell you, and what do you need to do?"

Kat also uses her dreams in important ways:

I go into dreams with questions or with requests. Since my father died, it's been amazing. For a while I felt clearly connected to his spirit, and I had very strong impressions of where he was and what he was doing and how he was sailing through the stars on his sailboat and sweeping down to visit.

But then he got farther and farther away, so one night four months after he died, I asked to see how he was. The whole night my father and I were in this beautiful men's clothing store, and he was trying on Italian suits and fantastic ties. He was not a clothes man, but here he was trying on one outfit after another. He would go into the dressing room and come out in some fantastic outfit. He was being very funny and theatrical and showing off and parading around and saying, "See I'm fine—I'm great actually." I was just sitting in a chair like you do when you're advising someone shopping, just appreciating him, and we were cracking jokes, and it was just great.

I probably saw twenty-five outfits and my dad in sort of a different aspect with each one, and I said, "Thank you, I got it."

I wanted to see him and I saw him. He's okay.

Padi dreamed of her grandmother a few months after her death. In her dream, she and her mother were riding on a train, and suddenly her grandmother appeared sitting across from them. Padi collapsed into her lap, crying and telling her how much she was missed and loved. After the tearful reunion, Padi sat up and asked her grandmother, "So, what's it like to be dead, anyway?" Her grandmother smiled, clasped her hands together in excitement, and exclaimed, "It's absolutely fantastic! It's better than Disneyland. You meet the most marvelous people on this side!" The dream comforted Padi, knowing that her grandmother was fine, wherever she was.

The more you focus on remembering your dreams, the easier it will be to recall them. Learning to tune in and receive these metaphoric messages takes practice, just as interpreting and decoding the dreams do. Using your dreams to unlock inner knowledge, the ultimate mind power, is an ancient art that anyone who really cares to learn can master. Many visual artists paint the images that come to them in their dreams. Dreams are a valuable source of creative inspiration that can lead to the joyful expression of your innermost self.

We do not have to be passive recipients of our brain-stem telegrams. We can begin to tap into the power of our dreams to receive valuable guidance and inspiration from our inner mentor. Sometimes it takes a few nights of sleep—or naps, if your lifestyle affords you that luxury—to dream the answer, but rest assured, the answer will come. And, like Robert Louis Stevenson, if you are dissatisfied with the response you receive, by all means, try again.

8

Mental Rehearsal

If one is lucky, a solitary fantasy can
totally transform one million realities.
—MAYA ANGELOU

Athletes know it, successful business executives know it, peak performers in every field know it. We become what we think about. The pictures we create and play in the movie theater of our mind are, to a very large extent, the sneak previews of our future. Mental rehearsal, or creative visualization, is a powerful technique when used to envision creative solutions, realize your dreams, and design a more joyful, satisfying life. There's an old saying that what a person can conceive can be achieved. Frank Lloyd Wright said: "The thing always happens that you really believe in, and the belief in a thing makes it happen."

By picturing ourselves creating at our highest levels, imagining the finished product and the deep joy that comes from creating, we move closer to our dreams. Visualizing the end result from our creative effort helps us achieve it. Can you imagine a painter being able to execute a masterpiece without knowing in her mind what the painting will look like? By picturing yourself reaching your creative goal, or just enjoying the experience of creating, you will progress more easily and naturally.

How you talk to yourself, the beliefs you hold about who you are and what you can do, shape your reality. You are only limited by the self-portrait you hold in your mind. By repeatedly imagining yourself accomplishing your goal, pathways seem to open up, opportunities arise serendipitously, and you find yourself living your life out loud.

> **W**e are what we think.
> All that we are arises with our thoughts,
> With our thoughts we create the world.
> —BUDDHA

Mental rehearsal, creative visualization, or picturing perfection is the simple but powerful act of creating in your mind an image of what you want. Done repetitively, this technique produces extraordinary results. When you assume a positive or negative attitude or picture, you get a positive or negative result. There are few accidents; most things happen in direct accordance with cause and effect.

> **W**hen I look into the future, it's so bright it burns my eyes.
> —OPRAH WINFREY

Mental pictures, repeated and converted into action by energy and faith, have enabled great leaders, inventors, artists, and other achievers to succeed in reaching their creative goals—in many cases, against all odds.

> **I**f you think you can, you can. And if you think you can't, you're right.
> —MARY KAY ASH

Many professional performers, including most athletes and speakers, mentally prepare before they go on. Heavyweight champion Muhammad Ali would program "future memories" of fights into his mind in preparation. Trial attorney Clarence Darrow mentally prepared himself the night preceding a big trial. The creative yet simple act of painting pictures in their minds propels mental rehearsers to success.

Dr. Charles Mayo, for whom the Mayo Clinic was named, would mentally rehearse the night before an important surgery; in his mind's eye, he would go through the procedure, step by step, from donning his surgical garb to the first incision.

If you can dream it you can do it.
—WALT DISNEY

Artists and craftspeople also use this technique to work on their creations. Contractor and cabinetmaker Michael Eschenbach always creates real-life three-dimensional pictures in his mind before he makes a drawing on paper. According to Michael:

> If it doesn't look right in my mind, then I mentally correct it before doing any drawing. As I'm driving from job to job, I visualize the state of the project and the steps coming up so when I arrive at the job site, I'm prepared for any question my clients or carpenters might have. I practice in my mind, and when I come across problems, I solve them in my mind instead of on the job. This technique helps me remember parts that I might have forgotten because I see what's missing as I imagine the situation.

When Salli is writing, she doesn't always create at the computer. Salli explains:

> I sometimes write while walking. What I do is rehearse what I'm going to write before I write it. I think it through, get some ideas, and then I start mentally doing my rough draft. When I get to the computer it's the second draft instead of the first.

Mental rehearsal can also be a powerful tool when it comes to changing unwanted habits. After his bypass surgery several years ago, CNN TV talk show host Larry King decided to use visualization to help resist "goodies" at holiday time and maintain a healthy heart. Whenever he is tempted to go off his diet,

King closes his eyes and pictures himself in the hospital after heart surgery. And mental rehearsal is not just for grown-ups. Children can do it with excellent results. Padi was teaching her six-year-old son to ride a two-wheeler, but he kept falling off the bike after riding only several feet. Noting his growing frustration, she encouraged him to stop, close his eyes, and picture himself riding straight and steadily past the point where he kept falling. Little Eli did this a few times and a moment later got back up on the bike and rode perfectly around the playground. He loves bike riding now, and, best of all, uses this valuable creative skill when facing other obstacles.

> In 1959 Liu Chi Kung, China's premier concert pianist, was arrested and imprisoned during the Cultural Revolution. Only a year earlier, he had placed second in the international Van Cliburn Tchaikovsky Competition. During the entire seven years he was held, this gifted musician was denied the use of a piano. Soon after his release, however, the pianist was back on a concert tour. With both admiration and astonishment, critics who observed him closely said his musicianship was better than ever.
>
> "How can you play so well?" one critic asked. "After all, you had no chance to practice for seven years." The musician's reply is memorable and instructive: "But I did practice—every single day. In my mind, I rehearsed every single piece I have ever played, note by note."
>
> —VICTOR M. PARACHIN

The reason creative visualization works so well is that the subconscious mind can't differentiate between what is real and what is creatively imagined. Research conducted at Stanford University demonstrated that a mental image actually ignites the nervous system in the same way as doing what was imagined.

According to brain physiology experts Dr. John C. Eccles and Sir Charles Sherrington, "When you learn anything, a pattern of neurons forming a chain is set up in your brain tissue. This chain, or electrical pattern, is your brain's method of remembering. So the subconscious cannot distinguish a real from an imagined experience; perfect mental practice can change, or correct, imperfect electrical patterns grooved there."

Because of this, mental rehearsal has been called one of the most powerful training strategies available for performing athletes. In fact, a recent study revealed that more than half of world-class gymnasts visualize their entire routine prior to competing.

> **Y**our thoughts can give you confidence, hope, and determination. You cannot think fearfully and build confidence. You cannot think of losing and expect to win. . . . Nor can you think of failure and expect success."
>
> —JAMES G. BENNETT AND JAMES E. PRAVIT,
> *The Miracle of Sports Psychology*

Mental rehearsal is not just for athletes, however. Professional speaker Lou Heckler also mentally rehearses in preparation for a presentation. A speaker for twenty years, Heckler is a highly respected, accomplished performer who has been the recipient of the highest honors in his profession. He says that all he needs to do before a presentation is run through the material a few times in his mind's eye, and that alone prepares him for success.

Salli tells of her own experience:

Unlike Heckler, I used to practice my material over and over with disappointing results. As presentation day grew closer, my anxiety would become overwhelming, and my creativity and humor would begin to shrivel. Even though I knew my subject and wasn't afraid of "being on stage," I just couldn't relax and have a good time. Far from being a joyful experience, giving presentations was rapidly becoming a nightmare. It was either stick with my writing and consulting and give up on being a presenter, or find a technique to pull me to another level. A friend suggested I use mental rehearsal and envision myself giving a dynamic and informative presentation where both the audience and I were relaxed and having a good time. Every night before falling asleep, and immediately upon awakening, I pictured myself at ease on stage and the audience adoring me. It worked! An instant convert to mental rehearsal, I now use this technique to help as I learn to write fiction, by picturing myself writing effortlessly and enjoying it.

EXERCISE

The next time you have to perform (physically or mentally), give creative visualization a try. Picture yourself succeeding brilliantly. See every detail, even what you are wearing. See the other people responding positively to you. Imagine how good you're feeling during and after the event. Do this exercise in a quiet place with your eyes closed, and do it at least three times before your "performance." This technique is especially effective if you mentally rehearse right before going to sleep and upon awakening.

Thanks to the encouraging results of a study completed in May, 1991, visualization is now beginning to be recommended for physical rehabilitation programs following surgery or prolonged immobilization as a way to speed recovery.

M. W. Cornwall and a group of researchers at the Louisiana Medical Center in New Orleans decided to see whether visualizing a workout could also improve strength, whether it could create "gain with no pain."

They used an exercise machine to measure the leg strength of twenty-four female subjects, and for three days half the women met in a quiet room for twenty-minute sessions and were told to imagine contracting their right thigh muscles. These sessions were electrically monitored to make sure the women didn't accidentally cheat by physically contracting their quadriceps. The control group of women neither exercised nor thought about it. When the researchers measured leg strength again, they discovered that when the visualizers actually lifted leg weights, they had increased thigh muscle strength by almost 13%; the control group showed no change. The researchers concluded that a mental workout appears to boost and strengthen a physical workout. This might prove to be a boon for people who are reluctant exercisers. Imagine just being able to mind-jog, or astrally aerobicise in your reclining chair and getting the same results as those who actually work up a sweat!

> **B**y the time we are thirty years old we have recorded millions of pictures of ourselves in our subconscious mind. Some of these pictures are real experiences we have had, while some have been created by our imagination and are experiences that never actually happened. The decisions we make, the thoughts we have, our reactions to our own behavior as well as the behavior of others are determined by these pictures.
>
> —LYN PFAELZER

Through your imagination you can experience the pleasure of achieving your goal, and that is a wonderful motivator as you become more and more attuned to your creative essence. By taking some time every day to picture yourself having what you want, doing what you want, feeling the way you want, you will actually be developing a subconscious blueprint for your future joy and success.

According to Dr. Paul R. Surburg, Department of Kinesiology at Indiana University, mental rehearsal, also called mental practice or imagery practice is not a new concept. At the turn of the century, there are anecdotal accounts of individuals utilizing this type of mental activity to enhance physical or motor skill performance. Most studies (and there are at least 100 studies) have reported that a combination of physical and mental practice is an effective method for learning or improving physical skills.

Recently several studies have been conducted in China (Zhang *et al.*, 1992) and in the United States (Gray, 1990) where mental rehearsal was combined with videotaped modeling. One study implemented mental imagery training with videotaped images to enhance table tennis skills of seven- to ten-year-old children. The study conducted in the United States found mental rehearsal with videotape modeling a very effective method to improve racquetball skills of college students. A study by Surburg found mental practice to be effective with elderly individuals. It is obvious that all age levels may benefit from the use of imagery practice.

9

Let Nature Nurture You

Thousands of tired, nerve-shaken, overcivilized people are beginning to find out that going to the mountains is going home,
that wilderness is a necessity, and that mountain parks and res-
ervations are useful not only as fountains of timber and irrigat-
ing rivers, but as fountains of life.

—JOHN MUIR

Getting back in touch with nature helps you reconnect with
yourself and your creative spirit. Just getting outside to a
change of scenery revitalizes and refreshes you. Nature is the
most creative force there is, and by reconnecting with and honoring it, you can deepen your relationship with your own creativity.

There is nothing more creative than nature. No artist could
create anything as beautiful. Artist Miller Phoenix doesn't consciously draw on nature, she "just lets it come through" her.

I let the blessings come through, I feel the energy or the
spirit of nature in everything. I think that's why I like to
take my walk three times a week—just to be out in nature.
If you're able to let yourself be part of it and not separate

106

from it, you can channel your energies more clearly. I believe if we keep ourselves separate from nature, we keep ourselves separate from our creative force.

Aboriginal peoples around the globe knew instinctively that nature was the fountain of life, understood intuitively the power of nature to transform, enlighten, energize, and heal. They realized they were not self-sustaining and that they needed to respect and care for the environment, that humans are part of an all-encompassing organism and that nature is not something outside of ourselves. As cultures became more civilized, people spent less and less time outside and began to forget how nature is inextricably entwined with survival— began to lose their awe and reverence for life.

In the Australian aborigine culture, initiation of a young girl involves developing the sensibilities and concentration that make her aware of her connection to the natural world. She is isolated for a period of time in which she is to focus all her attention on every sight, smell, and sound of her natural environment, which is believed to increase her life force and animation of her body. Aborigines believe that if the girl does not acquire the ability to fill herself with the spirit of nature, her eyes will dull, her hair will gray prematurely, and her body will become weak. They believe that early aging results from a loss of connection with the spirit of nature.

Although it should seem obvious that we are a part of and need nature, many of us have forgotten this vital link. It's as if we think we are above nature and were born to dominate her. Because of our need to control, and because we live in artificial ways, we have lost the way into nature. We have become estranged from nature, and this feeling of separateness is the major cause of our tragic environmental problems. According to Harper's Index, the average American spends less than 4% of his or her time outdoors.

The September/October 1992 issue of *Creation Spirituality* noted a survey by the Smell & Taste Foundation that found that people aged sixty-two and older associate nature smells (like hay, horses, and pine) with their childhood; while those aged twelve to sixty-one remember smells of plastic, scented markers, VapoRub, Sweet Tarts, and Play-Doh. Although plastic, scented markers, and Play-Doh have their place, the fact that we associate them with nature points to our estrangement not only from our environment but from our own authentic nature as well.

We cannot care for what we no longer know. When we try to put nature outside ourselves, to dominate and exploit her, we not only lose our individual creative energies, we jeopardize life itself. Just as our inner forces dwindle, our support systems languish. Although man is but a tiny part of nature, we have become like a bad case of poison ivy that refuses to heal. The more we scratch, the more the poison spreads.

> **A**udrey Shenandoan, Onondaga clan mother, writes in *Wisdomkeepers: Meetings with Native American Spiritual Elders*: There is no word for *nature* in my language. . . . Nature, in English, seems to refer to that which is separate from human beings. It is a distinction we don't recognize. This disconnection nature and its rhythms contributes to our disconnection with ourselves and those around us.

We have become disenfranchised from nature, uninvolved spectators. Some people have to travel miles from their homes to find solitude and silence. And even these green sactuaries are becoming harder to access. In California, for example, it's necessary to make a reservation months in advance for popular campsites.

Screenwriter and director Eugene Core connects with nature to recharge his creative batteries and describes just how vital the connection is to him:

> I don't thrive separated from nature for any long period of time. It amazes me how tense I get. You become unaware of the tension. If you put a frog in boiling water, it'll jump out. If you put a frog in tepid water and just gradually raise the temperature, it'll just stay in there and cook to death. We are all a version of the frog that gets cooked to death.

One day you end up in the woods, and you realize that you've been cooking yourself to death. You experience that sudden visceral physical change where everything loosens and opens up. And, then, only in hind sight do you realize what horrible shape you're in emotionally. It's easy to lose track of that.

An Hour a Day in Nature

In order not to "lose track of that," spiritual explorer Audrey von Hawley insists on spending at least an hour of every day outside.

> By spending time in nature, you get more tuned in, you begin to look, listen, and notice things you hadn't before. Nature is so beautiful, creative, and nonjudgmental, and when you get out into it, you become part of it. I always feel very nurtured and better than before I went outside. Spending an hour a day in nature sounds frivolous at first, because we think we should be doing something else, but it's been really very positive for me.
>
> As a culture, so much of our time is spent indoors. But the animal part of us needs to be outside to connect with the natural side of ourselves. For me, gardening, even walking the dog feels wonderful. Spending an hour each day in nature grows on you, it becomes something you *need* to do.

Albert Amateau, one hundred and five years old, says he expected longevity. "I lived my life in such a way that I knew I would live beyond one hundred," he explains. Being an avid walker has always been part of his life. He was once examined by an incredulous physician, fifty years his junior, who was amazed to hear that Mr. Amateau walked four or five miles every day. "What do you do when it rains?" asked the doctor. "I put on a raincoat," the old man replied.

Ruth Stotter agrees. "I'm the happiest when riding a bicycle or hiking on a mountain," she says. Ruth is fifty-five years old and is a beautiful, radiant woman in great shape, owing to her love of the outdoors. She counts among her most joyful moments when she first descends from a ski lift and looks out upon the mountains. Sometimes Ruth lies in bed at night and counts all the wonderful beaches she's visited.

Getting out into nature not only feels good, but it ignites the creative spark. Spending time in nature is one of the most effective incubation tools and reenergizers. A European engineer was taking a walk in the forest one day when a burr attached itself to his jacket and the idea for Velcro popped into his head. David L. Stidolph is the vegetable marketing wizard who introduced a new way of packaging broccoli—in florets. He explains that his best ideas come to him when he goes and sits on a certain rock in the Sierras. Anytime he is working on a creative project, he heads to the mountains for inspiration.

Padi's great-grandfather, a painter and air-brush artist who lived in New York City, knew the importance of the outdoor experience to fuel his creative fires. Each day, three hundred and sixty-five days a year, no matter what the weather was, Maurice Kassel went horseback riding in Central Park first thing in the morning, before he settled in to paint. He lived to the age of eighty-six and painted until the day he died.

In addition to providing the perfect creative incubation environment, part of the magic of nature is the healing effect it has on us. In a recent study by University of Michigan psychologist Rachel Kaplan, just having a window at work with a green view reduces stress, increases productivity and job satisfaction, and improves morale and worker health. Workers whose views include scenes of nature reported less frustration and more enthusiasm with their jobs. The study reaffirms that Mother Nature soothes the brain and provides relief from mental fatigue, which paves the way for creativity.

Salli tells how when she was three, she had a running battle with her parents that went like this:

"Put your shoes on right now, Salli Ann." "But, Mom, it feels so good." "Your feet will grow big and wide; do as I say." "Ah, Dad, please." "You will get tape worms if you don't wear shoes, put them on this minute." "But it tickles my toes." "NOW."

I went barefoot at every opportunity and still do. I find comfort in connecting with the earth. I have a passion for the land that is as strong as a passion for a lover. It feels unnatural to me to be indoors, and I have to discipline myself to stay inside, especially when the sun shines. To me all things spring from mother earth. Nature is the wellspring of creative inspiration.

The more we connect with the earth, the more we care for our natural environment and the more we feel nourished in return. Knowledge of the restorative healing power of nature is not new. For centuries, Chinese aesthetics have meditated upon miniature gardens set up in pottery bowls inside their houses as a way to establish harmony between their inner and outer worlds.

Every time I pull up a wildflower, I find it connected to the universe.

—JOHN MUIR

Dr. Bowen F. White, an internationally recognized stress expert in Kansas City, Missouri, uses this ancient knowledge of nature's healing power to help his patients. He recommends that they spend time in nature as often as they can, as a way to reduce stress and enhance creativity. He has even produced audiocassette tapes using guided imagery to take patients on a trip to the mountains or the beach, where they can experience deep relaxation.

"Many listeners have found that using guided imagery takes them away from their present circumstances long enough for them to find peace, renewed energy, and a sense of healing. Anyone facing a challenge—physical, mental or spiritual—will find these journeys to be a welcome guide," he says.

Numerous biofeedback studies affirm that when patients envision restful, natural settings, meditative states are produced that can actually reduce the physiological effects of environmental or self-inflicted stress.

EXERCISE

After a particularly stressful day, sit quietly where you can be assured of no interruptions. That may mean turning off the phone and telling family members or roommates to leave you alone for twenty or thirty minutes. Loosen your clothing, and sit in your most comfortable chair or lie down in bed. Close your eyes and think about the most beautiful natural setting you've ever experienced. What setting moved you the most? Was it a sunset spilling over a tropical island? A field of golden poppies? A secluded beach in midwinter? The Grand Canyon at dawn?

Search your mental scrapbook and go to this special place. Let your imagination take you on a journey there by yourself. See yourself in your special place. Try to remember what you were wearing, how the sky looked, what the earth beneath your feet felt like. What was the temperature like? Were you aware of any smells in the air? Try to recreate the scene with all your senses. The more senses you can involve in this visualization, the more benefit you will receive from it. See yourself relaxed, joyful, just being there, feeling good. If any thoughts other than how beautiful this scene is enter your mind, imagine a large black felt eraser just erasing the thoughts away. Try to stay in this place, eyes closed, for at least twenty minutes.

If merely imagining a natural space can have a strong regenerative effect, imagine how much more healing it is to *be* in nature. Recent scientific evidence has shown that our brain chemistry actually changes when we go outside, and that's why getting out into nature feels good—because it *is* good for us.

Harness Those Ions

When we go outdoors, neurotransmitters in the brain respond to changes in the ions, tiny particles in the air. Ions carry positive or negative electric charges. Air rich in negatively charged ions appears to have a refreshing and stimulating impact. Negative ions have been shown to increase serotonin, the brain's neurotransmitter associated with more relaxed moods. Negative ions are found around waterfalls, clean mountain air, and beaches, but negative ions disappear in polluted urban areas or enclosed spaces.

A relationship has been suggested between depression and increased positive ions in the air. Some researchers think the trend for people to spend increasing amounts of time indoors in front of computer display terminals and TV sets, and under the partial spectrum of fluorescent bulbs, affects the incidence of headaches, arthritis, diabetes, hay fever, hormonal imbalances, and other maladies. Our lack of connection to nature may be affecting us more than we realize.

Over twenty-five years ago, the Air Ion Research Laboratory was established at the University of California, Berkeley, to study the impact of ions on living things. The lab has facilities for exposing plants, insects, bacteria, and small animals to measured amounts of small air ions in a controlled environment. A remarkable body of new information is emerging, based upon hard experimental evidence showing that these extremely tiny currents and voltages influence a wide variety of biological processes.

In one group of lab studies, negative ions had a lethal effect on a wide variety of molds and bacteria, including such dangerous organisms as those responsible for typhoid fever and cholera. In extensive studies with plants, negative air ions enhanced the growth rate of a wide range of vegetables and grains.

All this research has important implications for humans. Modern urban environments pose a threat to the ion balance in nature. Ion depletion from pollution, traffic-engendered smog, ducts of ventilation systems, and stray electrical fields can result in sleepiness, loss of attention, discomfort, and headaches. Restoration of ions to normal levels has reportedly reversed these effects.

Hipocrates, the world's first meteorologist and the father of medicine, noted in the fifth century, B.C., that certain winds had a negative influence on people. "The winds which must pass over mountains to reach cities," he wrote, "do not only dry, but also disturb the air which we breathe and the bodies of men, so as to engender disease." The suspicion that these "winds of ill repute" might involve air ions has been studied extensively in Israel, where the *sharav*, a complex weather characterized by a hot, dry wind, makes nearly 25% of the population ill.

Until the day comes when we all have negative-ion-producing machines in our homes, cars, and offices, and live in covered enviro-domes, the time we take daily to get out into nature will not only have soothing effects on the brain and nervous system, it may prevent certain types of illness as well.

EXERCISE

Try to spend at least thirty minutes or more outside each day, regardless of the weather. Taking a walk in a park can refresh you and clear your mind to make way for creative inspiration. Try taking a walk break instead of a coffee break, and see how good you feel. Invite a friend or co-worker. Instead of meeting friends or business associates for lunch, Salli and Padi often invite them to take a walk instead. We think better on our feet and find the time spent walking to be extremely energizing and creatively productive.

Most of us can begin to increase the amount of time we spend outside. For city dwellers, getting close to a waterfall or acres of country meadow can be a real challenge. Yet, taking only an hour's bus ride from most cities can fill the requirement of cleaner air, less traffic pollution, and more open space. Sitting on a bench listening to the birds or going barefoot in a park can make you feel better. Many cities are located near lakes or rivers, and just getting close to a body of water can give urbanites similar benefits. Taking a boat ride is a wonderful way to enjoy nature; even if it is around Manhattan's Statue of Liberty or on a paddle-wheel boat on the Mississippi in New Orleans.

Let the trees be consulted
before you take any action
every time you breathe in
thank a tree
let tree roots crack parking lots
at the world bank headquarters
let loggers be druids
specially trained and rewarded
to sacrifice trees at auspicious times
let carpenters be master artisans
let lumber be treasured like gold
let chain saws be played like saxophones
let soldiers on maneuvers plant trees
give police and criminals
a shovel and a thousand seedlings
let businessmen carry pocketfuls of acorns
let newlyweds honeymoon in the woods
walk, don't drive
stop reading newspapers
stop writing poetry
squat under a tree
and tell stories

—JOHN WRIGHT

Sensitiveness to nature is not a trivial trait. It touches the depths of personality, and tends to make a living unity of science, the sense of beauty, and religion. In the silence of the forest, in the peace of starlit night, in the quiet of woodland waters, the sensitive spirit feels awe, reverence, aspiration— escapes the tyranny of the immediate yet without concession to creed. Trembling shadows on quiet waters, the first glow of dawn, numerous hints of aesthetic design in the infinite variety of natural forms, touch the sense of beauty. The processes of life, every phenomenon of matter, spur one's mind to try to understand the world. And all these experiences tend to integrate the human spirit.

—ARTHUR E. MORGAN, *Observations: A Collection of Aphorisms*

========================**EXERCISE**========================

Call your local chamber of commerce or nearest visitors' bureau for a packet of information. Discover parks, beaches, or scenic drives in your area that you may never have explored or even known about before. Make a date to become a tourist in your own backyard and spend an afternoon outside in a new place, or one you haven't visited in a long time.

We don't want to give the impression that nature can only be experienced on a camping trip or that you have to go somewhere to enjoy it. There are two kinds of nature experiences: the everyday nature encountered within the boundaries of our neighborhood and workplace, and the more pristine nature most of us must travel to in order to enjoy.

In the first, you get involved in planting a garden or window box, watching the trees in the front yard or nearby park change colors, observe the squirrels, butterflies, birds, and other little creatures around you.

In the second kind of nature experience, you go somewhere to marvel at the majesty of nature, somewhere you can get away from humanity, lose yourself in your own thoughts, and immerse yourself in the beauty that surrounds you. There you take time to check out the intricacies of the fern at your feet, or look out over the mountain and enjoy the grandeur. Instead of taking nature for granted, this is a special time to become one with nature, to recognize that you are a part of it. That nature is not outside yourself, not something to be tamed and controlled—but enjoyed and treasured.

Nature provides us with a sustenance we can find nowhere else. The gifts of nature are many, and the more we enjoy, the more we come to appreciate her bounty. The benefits of good health, stress reduction, physical exercise, and creative rejuvenation are just too great to miss by spending all our free time cocooning in our living rooms or socializing indoors.

The more we get out in nature to celebrate its abundance, the more we learn to revere all of life and the more creative ways we will discover for taking care of the earth and each other. Whenever we open up new avenues for creativity, our entire lives become enriched and more joyful.

OVERCOMING
THE
JOY CRUSHERS

> Life is a great big canvas, and you should
> splash all the paint on it that you can!
> —CAROLE RAE, *artist*

It's easy to become overwhelmed and lose a sense of control when obstacles to joy and creative expression seem to be everywhere you turn. The frantic pace of society, financial pressures, and the information explosion are toxic deterrents to living your life out loud. The work we do often *doesn't* work, and the way we complicate and burden our lives worrying about what others think often leads us to conform to social norms that gnaw away at our creative spirit and diminish our joy. The end result is stress and the neglect of our most important relationships with ourselves, our families, and our friends. When you feel victimized and out of control, your creative energy is sapped and joy fades.

You can eliminate these obstacles by taking back your life and your time, closely examining the choices you make and, most importantly, the changes you are ready to make to live your life out loud. We guarantee that after considering the impact these joy crushers have on your life and after completing the exercises in this section, you will gain more time and energy to explore and express your creativity. When you do this, your creative fruit ripens, and then, only then, will you harvest joy in abundance.

Imagine your life as a work of art, and you as the artist. What you choose to put on the canvas is completely up to you. The colors, shapes, depth, and light are in your power to create. The painting you end up with is nobody's creation but your own. Will you paint by numbers what someone else has penciled in on the canvas, or will you make your own decisions about which colors go where? Will you let others barge into your studio and finish the painting for you, or will you do it all

121

yourself? The choices you make about how to create your work of art will determine the beauty and depth of the final picture.

EXERCISE

How does the creation of your life look to you right now? If your life were represented on a canvas, what would the painting look like? Close your eyes and think about it for a moment. What colors or images come to mind?

Did you like what you saw? Were your colors bright, or dark? Were the lines flowing or jagged, vibrant or subdued? What message did your "painting" give you?

Whatever you imagined, remember that your work of art is not complete. As an unfinished canvas, it can change dramatically. You can choose to make it more interesting, more beautiful. The more thoughtful your choices, the more unique and powerful your painting will be. Like art, a beautifully created life comes from realizing you have choices and taking action on the best ones. When you are on target with your goals and life, your capacity for creative expression and the joy that follows are enhanced.

That is a powerful principle about joy—the more you take control of your life, the happier you will be. It's that simple. Researcher Angus Campbell, summarizing the University of Michigan's nationwide surveys on happiness, noted: "Having a strong sense of controlling one's life is a more dependable predictor of positive feelings of well-being than any of the objective conditions of life we have considered." Another study by Yale psychologist Judith Rodin found that increasing people's control over their lives improves health and morale.

When you stop living by the "shoulds" and "ought tos" and start living by what feels best and right to you, your self-esteem soars, your ability to thrive grows, and you begin to feel more courageous about taking risks. When you take control of your life, only then can you begin to experience more joy.

Awareness is the first step to living your life out loud. We have identified the following twenty-three blocks to creativity. Which ones get in your way? By identifying how and where you get stuck, you can begin to unravel the web of obstacles in your life that prevent you from achieving your optimal joy and creativity.

WHAT BLOCKS CREATIVITY?

Self-Defeating Beliefs
1. Fantasy and reflection are a waste of time.
2. Playfulness is for children only.
3. Problem solving is serious business; no fun or humor is allowed.
4. Reason, logic, numbers, and practicality are good; feelings and intuition are bad.
5. Tradition is preferable to change.
6. I am not creative.

Self-Imposed or Emotional Blocks
7. Fear of failure.
8. Inability to tolerate ambiguity and hang out until the best solution can be developed.
9. Inability to relax or take time out.
10. Excessive zeal to succeed quickly.
11. Lack of persistence.
12. Stress or depression.
13. Poor health habits: high-fat diet, insufficient exercise or sleep.

Work Obstacles
14. Lack of cooperation and trust among colleagues.
15. Autocratic management.
16. Too many distractions and easy intrusions.
17. Lack of acknowledgment or support of ideas and putting them into action.
18. Wrong livelihood.

Intellectual or Expressive Blocks
18. Lack of or incorrect information.
19. Inadequate skill to express or record ideas (verbally, visually, mathematically).

20. **Lack of intellectual challenge.**

Societal Pressures
21. **Bombardment of information and pressure to keep up—Infoglut.**
22. **Acceleration of the pace of life and time—Lifespeed.**
23. **Addiction to consumerism.**

10

Work Creatively

The trouble with the rat race is even if you win you're still a rat.
—LILY TOMLIN

Having meaningful employment is basic to living a fruitful, creative life. Work can be just a dead-end job with seemingly little connection to who you are and what matters to you. Or it can be challenging, stimulating, and joyful. Your work can mirror your values and provide a reflection of who you are. Or it can be a place where you count the minutes until it's over.

Work is central to your life. From our research and interviews, the evidence is overwhelmingly clear—people who engage in work that is meaningful feel it is one of the most rewarding areas of their lives. They look forward to each day knowing they are appreciated, productive, creative, contributing members of society.

> **H**umans have a basic need to express their essential values and talents in their work. Your work is your way of participating in creating a better world. It is your vehicle for finding your unique right place in the human family. It is an antidote to alienation and loneliness.
>
> —SUSAN CAMPBELL, *From Chaos to Confidence: Your Survival Strategies for the New Workplace*

125

Uniting who you are with how you earn your living opens up an exciting, creative world, a vitally enriching part of your life. Just putting in your time to pay the bills is at best limiting and at worst stifling, stressful, and dangerous to your health.

Exercise instructor Joan Price, has created the work that works for her while helping to create a better world:

> My work is play. My play is work. Most people go to work, and then afterward they have leisure. But I looked at my life at a certain point and said, How do I make what I love to do my work? Instead of making time for it as my leisure. That doesn't mean it's always fun. There are lots of things about it that are very hard, and I have to plod along to get them done.
>
> After recovering from my near-fatal accident, I decided that I wanted to share the joy of movement. Once I was able to move, think, and write again, . . . then I knew that whatever it is that I'm able to do now and whatever it is that I almost lost by losing my life, I have to give back to other people. I felt like I had a mission to give that back. And so I educate people through my writing and through my classes and one-on-one instruction, and I have a full and wonderful life. I'm ecstatically joyful! I was no real slouch before, but it makes a difference, almost dying. It changes everything.

The Rat Race

Most Americans anticipate the weekend much as someone wandering in the desert lusts after a cool drink of water. And just like in the movies, more often than not, the oasis turns into a mirage. The cultural model is that most of us are locked into existing from weekend to weekend, squeezing in what we *really* care about during our nonworking hours. Yet, Saturdays are usually jammed packed with chores and "to do" lists. There's grocery shopping and car maintenance and weeding the garden and doing the laundry and cleaning the house and fixing what's broke. What doesn't get done on Saturday awaits us Sunday morning. It's not that these activities aren't rewarding, it's that there are too many tasks to savor any of them. If we aren't doing rewarding work, our lives can feel like a rat race.

We tend to operate on delayed gratification, propelled along by the hope and promise of "someday." There is little time for relaxing on the weekend, and then it's back to the same old grind. Add this to the stress of spending eight or more hours a day cut off from ourselves, and we are a nation whose poor health and spiritual anxiety are escalating. It's tragic but true that the average American male dies within twenty-four months after he retires from his life's work. This is a good statistic to keep in mind if you are torturing yourself with work that is stressful and unrewarding, waiting for the big payoff called retirement.

Working More and Enjoying It Less

A study published by the National Institute of Standards and Technology in Maryland found that the annual time spent on the job by an average adult in the United States rose by 86 hours between 1969 and 1989. Juliet Schor reported in *The Overworked American* that employed Americans spend 163 hours more per year on the job than they did in 1969.

More Americans than ever before in history have a second job. No wonder Americans are more pressed for time than ever, more rushed, more scheduled, and more hassled. And as a result, less joyful. These statistics are made all the more vivid as 82% of Americans say they do not "find their work rewarding" according to a Roper Organization survey.

Michael Phillips is a classic example of what can happen when work takes over your life. At the tender age of thirty-one, Michael was a rising star in the banking business. He was one of the youngest vice presidents of a major U.S. bank. A stressed-out overachiever, Phillips had never taken a vacation in his adult life. The following is a brief account of what happened when a client sent him on a cruise:

> Once I was on board and realized that there was literally nothing to do, I just about had a nervous breakdown. I even tried to get a helicopter to come pick me up. Finally,

I was faced with the choice between going insane and just sitting in a deck chair and looking out at the ocean for several days straight. It was the beginning of a big change for me, a big change in the way I thought about myself, about money, and about the world. In the banking world and in the business world, money is the name of the game. But once I thought through *why* I felt so driven to make money, I realized that my job was keeping me from getting what I *really* wanted.

What I *was* getting was hemorrhoids and stress ulcers. A psychiatrist I consulted helped me see that I was using stress to make me more effective in the business world, and that same stress was making me sick. And the more money I made, the sicker I was getting.

Michael was a victim of adrenaholism, better known as stress addiction. Being hooked on the stress chemicals our brains emit keeps us from initiating changes in our lives that can make us feel better. The addict requires more and more of these neurohormones to achieve this stress high. We can either become addicted to the stress and depression chemicals in our brain or retrain the brain to become addicted to the joy chemicals.

Fortunately, it is possible to stimulate endorphins, the chemicals that lead to the joy response. Wouldn't you rather become hooked on joy? By making a conscious daily effort to put more joy in your life, you can reduce stress and replace it with a happier and healthier alternative.

That's what Michael did. His crisis forced him to rethink his life, slow down the pace by getting out of the fast lane, and regain his health. He quit his high-stress job to work as the business manager of a non-profit foundation, where he could set his own hours and work on projects that had greater personal meaning to him. By reducing the stress from his work schedule, Michael freed up time and energy to pursue community service activities and write books. These activities fed his spirit and stimulated his creativity.

For most people, switching careers in mid-life is frightening. However the stressful pace that you find exciting or at least tolerate in your youth often becomes unacceptable and unhealthy as you grow older and your priorities change. Some no longer need to prove to themselves that they can put in twelve-hour days or beat the sales quota every month; others just get worn out, and the warning signs of physical breakdown motivate them to seek healthier work.

Like Michael and others who seek more balance and joy in their lives, you must be willing to admit when your work life isn't serving you and then have the courage to change it creatively.

> Life has a way of accelerating as we get older. The days get shorter, and the list of promises to ourselves gets longer. One morning we awaken, and all we have to show for our lives is a litany of 'I'm going to,' 'I plan on,' and 'Someday, when things are settled down a bit.' "
>
> —ERMA BOMBECK

According to Brad Edmonson in the July/August 1991 *Utne Reader,* 64% of people aged twenty-five to forty-nine say they fantasize about quitting their jobs to live on a desert island, travel around the world, or do something else for enjoyment. We feel it's a scandalous waste of human potential that 95% of the working population say they do not enjoy the work they do and put their time in solely for the money. It's no surprise that more Americans die at nine o'clock on Monday morning than at any other time.

Although more and more people are coming to realize that the stress and energy sap of working at jobs that don't suit them is at best a waste of resources—and at worst literally killing them—it usually takes considerable courage to risk change. It requires an entire shift in perspective to believe that you can meld your spiritual ideals with your work, your personal and political ideals with your source of income. Yet few things impact your life more positively than finding the work you are meant to do.

> There is only one success—to be able to live your life in your own way.
>
> —CHRISTOPHER MARLOWE

Consider this: You spend at least a third of your adult life working. More than any other activity, work defines who you are. In a very real sense you become the work you do. You can't be a cutthroat, callous businessperson during the day and a loving, empathic companion at night. You are literally shaped by the work you choose. Clearly, if you are to live life joyfully and creatively, it's paramount to create work that is harmonious with your entire life. Work that helps you learn how the world works. Work that enhances who you are and who you can become.

> **I** work to create a sort of canvas, a place where beauty is allowed to happen. I love my work because it doesn't feel like work at all; there is no separation between the work I do and who I am. I have found the work I am supposed to do—where my passion, my work, and my joy are one and the same.
>
> DOUG GOSLING, *master gardener*

How we admire people who derive personal satisfaction and sustenance from their work! It is a myth that only extremely fortunate people will ever manage to find work that is fulfilling—and one the authors have worked to dispel for over two decades. **With perseverance you *can* find or create the work that is right for you.**

> **A**ccording to author Elizabeth Kübler-Ross, the most common regret of the terminally ill is: "I made a living, but I never really lived."

Clarify Your Values

One of the most important considerations in creating meaningful work is to clarify your own personal values. What do you value most and what are your priorities?

John Parry, who owns a company that installs solar hot water systems is an example of someone who has figured out what's important in his life and created a work niche that fits him:

There are times almost every day that I get this little chill that runs through my body and I go . . . wow! . . . I'm really enjoying this day . . . I'm having a good time . . . I made some money . . . I'm in control of my life doing what I want to do, not what someone else wants me to do. What more could you ask for? I feel like I've gotten to a place I've always wanted to be. It's great. Sure, I could make more money if I went to work for Hewlett-Packard or something like that, but why? The money is not what it's all about. For me at least. It's about having that feeling every day. Where you're driving down the road, and you're sitting there thinking, I'm as happy as I can be, and I'm working. I'm being a productive member of society and enjoying it and getting paid for it.

Sara Alexander, a psychotherapist who helps people focus on themselves—"which is where the source of creativity and joy is"—is another example of someone who had designed her work to fit her values. She describes a bit of her philosophy about her work as a therapist:

I think creativity is inside people's hearts and souls. I believe my work is helping people see what gets in the way of focusing on themselves, and I think when I'm successful, their lives become more joyful and creative. Other things happen, too. They have more intimacy in their lives and more closeness. One couple . . . went from planning their divorce to redecorating their house. They kind of cited that as an example of why they would never be able to separate—We can't leave each other because we're redecorating. That's a co-creative process . . . something that both he and she can do together, and I get to watch it.

Gifted are those who find ways of alchemizing an interest into a livelihood and who continue throughout their lives to cross-pollinate curiosity and work in ways which nurture both. Rarely are such people wealthy—for wealth usually requires the sale of one's time and personal concerns for those of the marketplace—but often they can find or create a sanctuary of

financial safety: poets who teach, readers who own book-
stores, artists who design clothing, mountain climbers who lead
expeditions. It is possible the most socially valuable work
comes from those who refused, at some critical juncture in
their lives, to give up their interests for the open market, and
instead determined to find a way to engage the whole self in
meaningful work, for they give us back poetry, stories, music,
paintings, and a view from the top of the mountain.

—MICHAEL PHILLIPS and CATHERINE CAMPBELL, *Simple Living Investments*

Creative Options

Both John Parry and Sara Alexander are part of the growing
community of one-person business owners. There is good reason why the one-person business is the boom industry of the
1990s; it's a business form that allows for maximum freedom
of expression and the greatest degree of personal working au-
tonomy. Running a one-person business has become one of the
most significant social revolutions in America today. Not only
does it allow you to respond effectively to the increased insecurity in the workplace, it allows you to create meaningful work
that parallels what is important in your life.

For those who feel life is more than making money, the one-
person business is an exciting business form. It is business as
lifestyle—business as a statement about who you are and what
you value.

—CLAUDE WHITMYER AND SALLI RASBERRY, *Running a One-Person Business*

However, you don't have to own your own business to create the right work situation for yourself. Sometimes the work
you are currently doing is right for you, but the hours are too
long, the commute too far, the stress too much, your life way
out of balance. Here is an opportunity to flex your creative
muscle. (You might want to review Chapter 4, "Risk to Grow,"
at this point). Increasingly, people like yourself are designing
creative solutions to keep their work and personal lives healthy,
and business owners are realizing that when workers are
healthy, the company will also flourish.

Our friend Lynn is an example of someone who knows her priorities and is willing to risk asking for what she wants and investing the time to help make it happen. Lynn was a department manager for a health insurance company when she became pregnant with her second child. She decided that working five days a week didn't give her enough time to be with her family. She knew that working four longer days would suit her better, and although there was no precedent for that type of schedule at her company, she approached her boss with the idea. He agreed to try the new arrangement on a trial basis, and after seeing how well it worked, agreed to change her schedule permanently.

Lynn has been working four longer days instead of five for two years now and is thrilled with the arrangement. She was able to keep a job she enjoyed and increase the amount of time spent with her family. She even began sewing again, a hobby she had abandoned years ago for lack of time.

"When I realized that I had stopped all the activities I enjoyed," Lynn recalls, "like sewing, knitting, swimming, and doing things with my kids, I thought, 'This doesn't make sense. What am I working for, anyway?' "

================ **EXERCISE** ================

If you had a magic wand, how would you change your work schedule to match your best inner rhythm and enhance the quality of your life?

Imagine what the perfect workday would feel like. Hour by hour, what would you do? How many hours would you work? What else would you include in your day besides work? What kinds of creative activities would you make time to pursue?

What steps could you take to incorporate some of these ideas into your life right now?

Lynn was a pioneer at her company; she was the first employee to work four ten-hour days a week rather than five eight-hour days. Flex hours and job sharing are not the kind of suggestion likely to come from your boss, so it's up to you to take the initiative. If flexible working schedules don't exist now where you work, it doesn't mean they will never exist. Someone has to take the first step. Why shouldn't that someone be you? Workplaces will never change unless the people in them are willing to push for change.

Of course, commitments and passions change; life is a continuum. The work that was right for you when you were twenty-five is not necessarily right for you at forty-five. And society is in a whirlwind of change, as Robert J. Kriegel and Louis Patler, authors of *If It Ain't Broke, Break It,* explain: "The current cycle of change is unprecedented in modern society. Within ten years, at least one fourth of all current 'knowledge' and accepted 'practice' will be obsolete. Within ten years, twenty times as many people will be working out of their homes. Two-career families will multiply: Currently one half of all families have two paychecks; this will become three quarters. If you are under twenty-five, you can expect to change careers every decade and jobs every four years, partly because you choose to and partly because entire industries will disappear and be replaced by others we haven't heard of yet. The forty-hour work week will become a dinosaur. We will work 20 percent more and sleep 20 percent less than we did a decade ago."

There are several other work options that we encourage — it's a matter of which one best fits your goals and needs at this time. Internship/apprenticeship, job sharing, telecommuting (working from home by phone, fax, and modem), working four-fifths time or less, and taking long amounts of time off are all becoming increasingly popular as people design new ways of organizing work.

A leave of absence is another strategy to prevent burnout and restore energy, creativity, and enthusiasm about work. An accounting firm we know allows the partners to take two-month summer sabbaticals every four years as a way to prevent burnout and let these hardworking professionals restore themselves. One partner took his family to Africa to live with a Masai tribe for a month; another traveled through Spain. Of course, during the traveler's absence, the workload is heavier on the rest of the partners, but they are willing to put in the extra effort, knowing that their time off will come soon, and that this arrangement promotes a healthier and happier company.

Whatever option you choose, the important point is to remain flexible, accept that the world is changing rapidly, and realize it's okay to ask for what you want.

When we spoke to Myrna she was desperate for a change but was so stressed out that she couldn't begin to see that she even had any options. Myrna commutes nearly four hours a day to a large city where she works in human resources. Leaving early in the morning and returning long past her family's dinnertime was wearing thin. The authors suggested telecommuting might be an option for her; at least part-time. The very idea of working one or two days a week from home was a luxury Myrna had not even allowed herself to consider, but her face lit up, and the concept really appealed to her. "But no one else is doing it," she said after only briefly considering the suggestion. "That may be because no one *asked!*" was our reply. We helped her write a proposal to the company including the benefits of telecommuting, and Myrna's company decided to give it a six-month trial period. Fair enough!

If you don't ask for what you want, chances are pretty good that you're not going to get it. It's like wanting to find a new primary relationship and staying home all the time, wondering why you're not meeting any new people! We can't understand why more people don't ask for and go after what they want— the worst that can happen is they won't get it. But at least they will have tried. And there are lots of benefits to be gained from planting seeds for our wishes to be granted in the future.

If You're Feeling Stuck

Some people feel they're in dead-end jobs. Even the most routine or seemingly dull job, however, can usually be made more interesting. If you're feeling stuck in a job right now, figure out ways to use the time as wisely as possible for your own growth and sanity as well as those of everyone around you. You never know, that dead-end job might just blossom into something special.

Here are some ways to make your job more interesting to you while making you more valuable to your company.

- Ask your boss what you can do to make his or her job easier—you may find new, more absorbing assignments coming your way.
- Spearhead a self-improvement support group with co-workers to increase teamwork and tackle problems more effectively. These could be learning meetings, where members each take on a project to study and report on to the group. The stimulation that results can reinterest you in your work, and by building stronger relationships with co-workers, make your work more enjoyable.
- Bring more of your creative self to work. Share your hobbies outside of work with co-workers. One woman we know is a gourmet baker who brought goodies to work every Monday morning. Her co-workers really appreciated the delicious gesture and were more receptive to her ideas and suggestions about the company as a result. By sharing her talent, she was able to shine at work.
- Invite frequent feedback and evaluation from your boss and/or co-workers. Asking others how you're doing, how you could improve, and what they think, can help you in your own personal development.
- Be proactive about making creative suggestions for ways to improve productivity, reduce expenses, or streamline procedures. Put these suggestions in writing to make more of an impact than offering them verbally. Find out what the biggest problems facing the business are, and start putting some of your creative effort toward coming up with innovative ideas.

EXERCISE

Describe the best job you ever had. What factors felt right? (i.e., the people, type of work, work environment, pace, etc.) What factors could be improved about your work situation right now? How could you bring more of your creativity to your job?

If you currently find yourself stuck in a job that's really unrewarding, and you can't make the shift just yet, try changing your perspective by developing a different attitude. Make converting an unfulfilling job into a challenge. While you are arranging things so you can take the risk for the work you want, or while you are discovering what work is perfect for you, make your present situation as rewarding as possible.

According to career guidance consultant Claude Whitmyer:

> When I counsel someone who is unhappy at work, I try to help them identify what's really going on. Sometimes it's an attitude adjustment, not a career adjustment. I've had clients who left professions and then after a few sessions together returned to those careers because they realized it was really their attitude not the career. Some people basically are into a general cycle of funk on the job. They go to work unhappy, which reflects on the work they do, and then the boss gets unhappy and then the co-workers, who have to cover for the unhappy worker become grouchy, and things become more and more miserable. Once the person realizes what is going on and makes a conscious attempt to infuse a little joy into the workplace, things begin to change.

The result, of course, is that their work improves; the boss becomes a bit more cheerful and in turn praises the employee. Their co-workers become happier and less stressed because they are not having to cover anymore, and everyone breathes a collective sigh of relief. As Claude tells his clients, "You may not be in the wrong job, you might just be in the wrong attitude."

Taking the Plunge

We can't emphasize enough that for a truly joyful life, it is necessary that you have meaningful work, that the greatest risk you can ever take is not to risk; that lifestyle is who you are, not what you have; that you can create the work that is appropriate for you whether you are self-employed or working for someone else. Yet, in these transitional economic times, we also know it's sometimes difficult to muster the courage to take career risks even when you know it's best for you.

Many people assume that earning a living by doing what they enjoy is an unobtainable dream, so they don't even try. Marsha Sinetar, the author of *Do What You Love, the Money Will Follow: Discovering Your Right Livelihood,* had difficulty making a shift into her right work. She admits, "I distracted myself with a respected career and with the inevitable promotions that came my way. I distracted myself even more successfully with an accumulation of material rewards and symbols of success. The unknown was too frightening to me; I couldn't conceive of doing what I knew I would love. My mind clung so desperately to the familiar."

It's never too late to be what you might have been.
—GEORGE ELIOT

Susan Campbell, corporate consultant, psychotherapist, and author, believes in taking frequent retreats to make sure her work continues to enhance her life.

I'm taking another look at who I am right now. I've taken periodic retreats during my career to see if I'm too identified with my roles and if my true self is expressed in my work. This is a luxury that most people don't give themselves.

Going on retreat helps you listen to your feelings and figure out what your cosmic vocation is, whether its entertainer or philosopher, teacher or fixer, whatever it is. If you bring that into your job description, you feel more whole when you're doing your work, and you don't get into as much of a split between am I working for "them" or am I working for "me." Self-employment is nice because you can structure your offering, your service, yourself. It gives you a certain freedom by creating or finding an environment that brings out your best self.

EXERCISE

Is self-employment an option? If you've ever considered being your own boss, what would your ideal business be?

Assemble a small group of peers who have opted for self-employment. Brainstorm with them about your business idea and how much money it will take to start a business, how long before you can expect a profit and other practical matters.

Marjorie, an employment agency executive for fourteen years, found her work becoming increasingly competitive and less enjoyable and knew she had to do something different but was skittery about making a change. When she started, there were four other personnel agencies competing in town. By the time she had burned out and bailed out, over thirty temporary employment agencies had sprung up in her market.

"When I first started, clients used to be loyal. I loved the work, I was so energetic. But as it got more competitive, loyalties disappeared, and it got a lot more difficult. It started to wear me down," Marjorie says.

A classic victim of job burnout, her stress and exhaustion made it increasingly challenging for her to function at work. "I'd drive to work and would just sit in the car for ten or fifteen minutes before I could get out. When I'd finally go in and look at my 'to do' list, I'd feel paralyzed," she recalls.

She continued this way for a year, worried that she was suffering from "a mental condition." Finally she quit, took a year off, and lived off savings. Recently she completed training as a masseuse, and she has happily gone out on her own and moved to a popular resort town with numerous spas where the need for her services should remain steady.

Gudrun Cable is another example of someone who ignored society's expectations and followed her own vision. She opened the Rimsky Korsakoffee House in Oregon serving up classical music, desserts, and coffee.

Instead of designing a place where other people are happy, I designed a place where I'm happy and other people like me are happy. I please only a small piece of the pie. I have no daytime hours, no rock and roll or country-western music, serve no liquor, and there is a no smoking policy.

Believe me, many people tried to discourage me from doing what I wanted because they felt it wasn't what the public wanted. When we started the coffeehouse twelve years ago, it was the first totally nonsmoking establishment in Portland. Everyone told me people wouldn't come and we would soon be out of business. I felt that if there was smoking, then I couldn't be there. Why open a business where you wouldn't enjoy being?

I don't know the meaning of the word 'drudgery.' I can't tell you the difference between vacation and work, and work and play. I also own another business, and I would rather be at one of my two places of business than anywhere on earth. When I'm going into either place, my heart starts beating faster because I love being there so much. When we open the coffee house, we light the candles and the music starts and I think it's the most beautiful place I've ever seen. That's the way it should be. That's what can happen when you don't compromise.

There is always another chance for you. You may have a fresh start any moment you choose, for this thing we call 'failure' is not the falling down, but the staying down.

—MARY PICKFORD

What do you do if you know your work situation isn't right for you, but you haven't a clue as to where to even begin sorting it all out? According to Norma Smith Davis, former career counselor turned organizational development consultant, it's not unusual for people to be unaware of what they do best, to feel shaky about beginning the search for their right work.

The way to find out what you really want to do is to pay attention to your feelings, your skills, and your talents. We do best what we enjoy most. Pay attention to what feels good, notice what particular things feel fun or satisfying. Remember, your work has to support your lifestyle. Many people expect the workplace, employer, or government to find them a perfect job and to keep them happy, satisfied, and challenged, but only *you* can do that.

People are born into the world without a clue as to what work they are best suited for or what work suits them best. Parents project their unfulfilled dreams and their goals or wishes onto their children, and many kids unquestioningly go along with these expectations.

After her car accident, Joan Price knew she no longer wanted to be a high school English teacher, so she saved a year's salary before beginning the transition into her current career as an exercise entrepreneur and author.

I wanted to see if I could make it as a professional writer. I knew I would also teach exercise classes, but I didn't think I could make a living just doing that. My plan was to see if I could make it writing, knowing that there would be this sort of apprenticeship. You can't just suddenly get in *The New Yorker!* You have to work at it and plod along and try things and realize you won't get accepted right away. So I thought that if I had a year, I wouldn't have to panic if I didn't make money. It was important to me not to be terrified. And not to have to back out two months into the experiment saying, "Oh, dear, I'm running out of money, I can't do this." Here I had this year, and it was like a paid scholarship to see what I could do with it.

I ended up being able to survive on my writing because I didn't have debts, because I was only responsible for myself, and because I was having such a good time with my new work that I wasn't needing other things that cost money.

EXERCISE

Make a list over the course of a few weeks. Think about what you truly enjoy, what makes you feel competent and content. Avoid being judgmental about your feelings. If you are currently employed, how can you incorporate some of these activities into your work?

The Career Development Profile below can help you determine your strongest skills and weakest characteristics. Take a minute to assess your current skill levels right now; you'll get valuable insight into what you like to do (where you check outstanding performance) and the areas you need to grow in.

The more your work mirrors your values, the more joyful and creative you will be. If there is a disparity between your core being and the work you do, or between your politics and those of the person or organization you work for, it will seep into your entire life like a slow poison. Too often as you progress in the wrong work you leave behind the things that are really important to you.

Creating the work that nourishes your life is one of the most rewarding paths to self-expression and joy.

> **To** be successful, the first thing you do is fall in love with your work.
> SISTER MARY LAURETTA

CAREER DEVELOPMENT PROFILE

	Check your current skill level			
	Outstanding Performance	Performing to Standard	Needs Improvement	Not Applicable
Planning / organizing	O	O	O	O
Communicating (upward, down, out)	O	O	O	O
Getting along with others	O	O	O	O
Negotiating	O	O	O	O
Time management	O	O	O	O
Speaking (meetings, presentations)	O	O	O	O
Writing reports	O	O	O	O
Problem solving	O	O	O	O
Creative initiative / innovation skills	O	O	O	O
Giving and receiving feedback	O	O	O	O
Selling yourself and your ideas	O	O	O	O
Handling conflict	O	O	O	O
Participating in community / civic activities	O	O	O	O
Project management	O	O	O	O
Knowledge of external trends / competition	O	O	O	O
Developing / coaching others	O	O	O	O
Supervising	O	O	O	O
Delegating	O	O	O	O
Other: specify				

11

Tame the Lifespeed Demon

Guard the senses and life is ever full . . .
always be busy and life is beyond hope.
—LAO-TZU

Your ability to experience joy by making time for creative expression is highly dependent upon the pace of your life and how you control it. The number of activities you pursue and personal and professional commitments you make determine your capacity for joy. Saying yes too much, and not setting clear limits for yourself and the people at work and home become obstacles to joy and inner peace. Unless you continually stay clear about what's in your 10% category, demands—coupled with wanting to please and accommodate others—will sidetrack you from the goals and activities that bring you pleasure and creative satisfaction.

It is harder than ever to be a human being on this planet. Never before have there been so many choices, distractions, interruptions, opportunities—in a word, changes. For millions of years, life went along pretty much the same on the planet. It has only been the past few hundred years that the pace of life has been so dramatically altered. According to Dartmouth professor of environmental studies Donella Meadows, in just the past twenty years, "almost as much damage has been done to the biosphere as in all human history before then."

The quickening pace of damage to the environment is symptomatic of the damage being levied on the human spirit. We are a species unaccustomed to the rapid changes brought about by the industrial revolution. We were originally built for hunting and gathering—taking long walks looking for berries, having hours to dig for roots with crude tools, waiting for the seasons to change to find the right healing herb for the new moon ceremony. Incubation and downtime were a natural part of life. Time for most of human history on the planet was real time—slow, uninterrupted, voluptuous time.

Prior to the industrial revolution, alternating patterns of stress and ease were normal human patterns. The jobs of a woodcutter, weaver, farmer, or shepherd had time out built into them. Certainly no phones, fax machines, or Federal Express deliveries interrupted the calm flow of work, the slow passage of time. The flow of work moved with the rhythm of the seasons. Planting time was followed by a slower pace, which picked up again at harvest time, when gathering, storing, and preparing food for the winter meant long, busy days followed by the storytelling quiet time of night. There was time for reflection, creative expression, and time to enjoy! Unfortunately, this healthier rhythm is not compatible with the demands and pace of life in the United States today. We are expected to go, go, go and keep up with a society addicted to overstimulation.

To experience quantum creativity, you need time out to unplug, reflect, catch your breath. You must create space in both your business and home lives to let joy in and creativity out. In order to best use your instinctive need for stimulation, you must curb your addiction to overstimulation.

It's not easy. Subtle factors in our environment contribute to the hectic pace we feel compelled to maintain. According to Ralph Keyes, author of *Timelock: How Life Got So Hectic and What You Can Do About It*, one seemingly small but significant casualty of today's time-pressured life is the pause. Word processors eliminate the need to stop and insert paper into a typewriter, microwaves mean watched pots *do* boil, call waiting on our phones interrupts the leisurely good-bye and eliminates any pause between calls.

"On a conscious level we may not miss these interruptions," writes Keyes. "We may have viewed them as nuisances. But they filled the day with brief respites. They gave our bodies a break. And the cumulative effect of eliminating any chance to catch our breath is to create a breathless society."

In Praise of the Pause

The lack of pauses compresses time in a way that is both physically and mentally exhausting, making us impatient and less able to shift gears to a slower pace. Keyes suggests reinstituting restorative pauses by sometimes doing things the long way, taking frequent breaks, alternating mental tasks with physical ones. As he points out, "Eliminating pauses is like eliminating the rests from a symphony or the descriptive passages from a book. You can get through books and music faster that way. But why would you want to?"

Jeff Davidson, author of *Breathing Space,* says, "At any given moment in your life, you can choose to drop back, take a deep breath, throw your shoulders back, look out the window, and contemplate something pleasant. In other words, you get to control the moment. No matter how hectic the particular circumstances appear to be, if you can just break through to that realization, then nothing can be that bad. People who don't do this will have lives that are much shorter and of less quality." In short, less creative and joyful.

It makes one rethink the ancient wisdom of siestas that is so deeply embedded in many cultures around the world, including those of Spain, Greece, and Mexico, to name a few. "Pausing" for several hours after lunch is easy to grow accustomed to, as many American tourists freely admit upon returning to their hurried lives at home.

TIME

Time doesn't exist for me; it melts. Can't keep watches on my wrist. They break, stop, slip off, disappear. I do not watch time; time watches me.

I think my soul was born so long ago that "now" lacks meaning.

Dr. Sprague locked his door against latecomers. Mornings spent with ear to keyhole chastened, but did not change, me.

I have been on time from time to time. I caught the midnight train to Venice, met my sweetheart under the clock at the Biltmore, pruned plantings when expected.

Time runs more slowly in hot climates. In California, Lucky Lou Lovedevine said, "Waiting for hippies is like bleeding to death."

Jonathan Z. Smith wrote a thesis on time that was brilliant, intricate, and a thousand pages long. He buried it. A lesson on time.

To understand the importance of time, watch carrots growing.

The minute that times a labor contraction, the minute that your lover takes to look at you, the minute that delivers hallucination or enlightenment, the minute between the blowing of the whistle and rumble of the train—these minutes are not time; they are the suspension of time.

What is happening now, now, now? Can't step in the same river twice; rivers, anyway, are for floating in.

—DELIA WHEELWRIGHT MOON

Everyone complains about time, but few of us do anything about it! We don't have enough of, it's passing too quickly, we're running out of it. As Jacob Needleman eloquently describes in *The Meaning Of Life,* "Everywhere, people are straining to set aside time for things that are felt to be humanly important—being with loved ones, enjoying nature, studying ideas, or engaging in some creative activity. And, more and more, it is becoming a losing battle. There is no issue, no aspect of human life, that exceeds this in importance. The destruction of time is literally the destruction of life."

Jeff Davidson agrees: "If people don't have the realization of how their time is being taken up a nanosecond at a time, they're liable to wake up one day and say, 'I'm not really enjoying myself.' "

This destruction of time has created a new cultural demon: Lifespeed. Lifespeed, the ever-increasing pace of life, is a major reason why so many people are so unhappy and stressed. Doing too much, too fast, too often is the curse of Lifespeed with its toxic by-product, stress. Stress is a stone wall we erect between ourselves and our inner joy. The good and bad news is that it is largely self-inflicted; bad news because of the toll it takes on our bodies and minds, and good news because we can do something about it.

EXERCISE

Stop in the middle of a "rush attack," when you're stressed to the limit. Take a deep breath and think about how you are feeling. Will what you are stressed about right now matter in five years? Five months? Five days?

Putting aside the emotional components of stress for a moment, the physical sensations alone seem to be the very antitheses of feeling joyful. The rush of adrenaline, sweaty palms, and increased rate of respiration make it impossible to feel joyful, unless the stress comes from hitting the jackpot or waiting for a loved one to come rushing off a plane.

The Stress Mess

Whether positive or negative, all stress makes us revert to instinct. We experience a number of physical reactions when we are negatively stressed beyond our normal limits. We have trouble concentrating; the thalamus gland secretes special enzymes that flood the bloodstream and shut down our senses. Blood leaves the brain and goes into the extremities to prepare us for the "flight or fight" response. Our peripheral vision increases, and rather than using both sides of our brain, we become more dominant on one side. An article entitled "Brain Cocktails," in the March 16, 1992, issue of *Forbes*, estimated that we temporarily lose up to 25% of our intellectual capacity when we're stressed out. Anyone who has ever been late for an appointment and then couldn't find the car keys has experienced this frustrating phenomenon. Being creative or joyful when you're in this stress survival mode is simply impossible!

If losing some of your brain power isn't bad enough, numerous studies have linked chronic stress to diseases such as heart ailments, ulcers, cancer, weak immune system, and depression. It's been estimated that as many as 15% of all Americans suffer from clinical depression. When United Way conducts surveys to determine human service needs in communities across the United States, they consistently find that people rank "depression and anxiety" as the number one problem in their lives.

Although some stress is considered healthy, most Americans have more than a healthy dose to deal with. Researchers have found that even though anxiety and the stress response can kill you in the long run, they actually make you feel good temporarily. Worrying, hurrying, hassling, and feeling impatient result in brain chemical changes that make you feel aroused and high, feelings you easily get used to and comfortable with.

The stress high is a tool that some people use for an edge in business. This high is illusory, can cause emotional and physical sickness, and actually prevents people from achieving the very things they are striving for.

Ironically, the technology of fax and answering machines, E-mail, cellular phones, and networked computers that promised to save us time and make our lives less stressful only contributes to the urgency we feel to respond and "be on" at all times. One would think with all these high-tech "conveniences," we would be putting in shorter work days and enjoying more leisure time. Sadly, just the opposite is true.

With the pace of society spiraling frenetically, joy will become increasingly elusive unless you seek it out by taking conscious control of your life, your time, and your priorities.

Ponder the irony of our desperate pace of life exemplified by this story of spiritual shortcuts. For centuries, religious Jews have made pilgrimages to Jerusalem's Wailing Wall, considered to be Judaism's holiest shrine. According to Jewish tradition, the spirit of God is in the wall, and written prayers slipped into the chinks between its huge old stones will be fulfilled. But in 1993, Avner Ocadia, deputy manager of marketing for Bezeq, Israel's state-run telecommunications company, decided that everyone "needs better access to God." So he launched a fax-God service. For no other charge than sending the fax, anyone anywhere can whisk off a prayer to God, which Bezeq employees gather daily and put in the wall's crevices. Over ten thousand heaven-bound faxes arrived the first year the service was offered.

Put Time on Your Side

The only antidote to chase away the Lifespeed Demon is to take charge of your time. When you stop being a victim of time, when you take charge and put time on your side, you transform the quality of your life exponentially. Instead of focusing most of your attention on the future, or worse yet, the past, learning to be in the moment—conscious of right now—is the first step in getting a handle on the quality of your time. By refining your awareness of the moment, being present and centered with yourself and others, you will automatically begin to slow down and get back in touch with the best balance of activity level for you.

Finding the best balance between stimulation and time out is the tricky part of it all. It's different for everyone. Just as one type of diet feels great to one person, the same diet would be repulsive to another. While stimulation is necessary for mental health, too much of a good thing is harmful.

There is more to life than increasing its speed.

—GANDHI

Time Out: CPR for Creative Hearts

Making time for time out can be difficult. But as you've seen, it is essential to the creative process. When you tune into your own rhythms and take time out to incubate and drift, you nurture your creativity. Time out is like CPR for creative hearts that have stopped beating or slowed down. By fine-tuning your rhythm of pause, do, pause, do, pause, do; you begin to balance your life, reduce stress, and feel healthier and more creatively expressive.

It takes practice to resist your conditioning to be perpetually busy and productive, methodically crossing off items on your "to do" list, fearing what might happen should you fail to have every moment filled up. Even for those who have reached their goals, making time for time out is a challenge.

"This is my fourteenth year in business," says investment counselor Roger Pritchard. "I've already made enough money and have enough savings to put my son through college. I've actually reduced my income and expenses from my business in order to create space to reinvent myself. I am learning to be intuitive rather than analytical. But not filling all my time up makes me anxious!"

Stressed spelled backward is *desserts*—which do you prefer?

The anxiety and discomfort of unscheduled time is too much for some. It's ironic that we humans are the only species on the planet that feel guilty about taking time out and relaxing. University of Vermont zoologist Joan Herberts found that the urge to hang out and unplug is natural and present in every species; only humans override this inclination to indolence. "Animal inertia" is essential for a variety of biological needs of the animal kingdom, including digestion, regulation of body temperature, even protection of the species. Americans work

1,957 hours a year, the French put in 1,646, and Japanese workers, 2,088. Contrast that with female lizards, who spend 97% of their day resting; walruses, who spend 67% of their day hanging out; and gorillas, who spend 51% of their time at rest.

TIRED

I've been working so hard you just wouldn't believe,
And I'm so tired!
There's so little time and so much to achieve,
And I'm tired!
I've been lying here holding the grass in its place,
Pressing a leaf with the side of my face,
Tasting the apples to see if they're sweet,
Counting the toes on a centipede's feet.
I've been memorizing the shape of that cloud.
Warning the robins to not chirp so loud,
Shooing the butterflies off the tomatoes,
Keeping an eye out for floods and tornadoes.
I've been supervising the work of the ants
And thinking of pruning the cantaloupe plants,
Timing the sun to see what time it sets,
Calling the fish to swim into my nets,
And I've taken twelve thousand and forty-one breaths,
And I'm TIRED!

—SHEL SILVERSTEIN, from *A Light in the Attic*

The Thirty-Minute Breakation

We're not proposing that everyone quit their jobs and emulate female lizards, but we are suggesting that relaxation time, temporarily unplugging from the frantic pace and daily responsibilities, is biologically necessary, and critical for emotional and physical health. Taking at least thirty minutes a day for quiet reflection will do wonders for your creativity and capacity for joy.

This time could be spent doing what feels good to you, listening to music, sitting in your favorite chair with your eyes closed, taking a hot bath, napping, going for a walk. The only rules are that the time should be spent by yourself and should not be mentally stimulating. Use this sacred time to pamper yourself, the way you would pamper a long lost friend who has come to visit. In other words, do unto yourself as you would do unto someone you cherish and love—like yourself!

Watching the news, reading, or talking on the phone is *off limits*. What we're going for here is unplugging, incubating, making space and time for downtime that puts no demands on your mind.

Some people may think it isn't possible to find thirty minutes a day for themselves. No matter how busy you are, you should be able to find the time, either by getting up earlier, going to bed later, taking a shorter lunch break, watching one less television program, spending less time on the phone, or eliminating one activity you do each day that brings you no pleasure. This daily time alone must become part of your 10% if you're going to make real, lasting changes in the quality of your life.

It often takes flexibility and creativity to make time for yourself. Jeweler and mother of three, Paula Brent leads a hectic life filled with family joys and obligations and still manages to find time for her creative projects. From the time she began having babies, Paula knew she needed time and space to herself to "survive." She created a small, private studio at home, and after the family has gone to bed, she does her creative work.

> It's a nighttime thing. When I try to work during the day, there're too many distractions. I get too fragmented. At night, it's like everything in the house is put to rest. Everything's in its place; everybody's sleeping; everything's fine, and I can pull the shades and go out and work and have long periods of time that are really focused. I recognized a long time ago that this was my survival. It makes a huge difference; it's feeding my soul.

You have to be willing to experiment with different schedules in order to create time for yourself, the way Paula does with her nighttime creative excursions. Or you can take time away from someplace else; a place that no longer serves your needs. Many highly creative achievers interviewed for this book sleep less than eight hours a day, or split their sleep time up unconventionally. Legend has it that Leonardo da Vinci slept several minutes every hour, twenty-four hours around the clock, rather than sleeping for hours at a time.

In addition to creating time, prioritizing the activities you're currently involved in can help you discover that it may be time to drop some things. It's easy to get locked into thinking you have to do everything you've been doing, and to forget about what really counts in your life. You can find at least thirty minutes a day to use in a better and more enriching, soul-feeding way. What daily thirty-minute activity can you get rid of, delegate, or combine with another task? Put these items on your 90% list!

EXERCISE

Make a master "to do" list; a list of everything you are committed to or involved in. Work, volunteer activities, spiritual and educational commitments, recreational and health activities, social and family obligations should be listed and then prioritized. Item by item, ask yourself; Is this an obligation or commitment that gives me satisfaction? What would happen if I stopped doing this altogether? Are there items on this list that someone else could handle for me? Look at the items on the bottom of your list. Can you let some of them go? What would happen if you stopped doing them or spent less time with them? Pulling out the lowest-priority items in your life will free up some time to spend in more joyful and creatively satisfying ways. You have 1,440 minutes to spend every day; spend wisely. By taking inventory in this manner, you will be able to re-shuffle your deck of obligations, throw out the cards that no longer work, and get a better hand. Throwing out the cards that don't contribute to your hand can be a highly empowering experience, plus it can free up relaxation time to get your creative juices flowing and bring more peace of mind and joy into your life. We often forget that our needs change, and what worked for us last year may no longer be healthy or productive.

Time is the coin of life. Be careful lest others spend it for you.

— CARL SANDBURG

EXERCISE

If you saved your appointment book or calendar from last year, you'll be able to get a quick and powerful picture of the quality of your time. Mark everything you did that was an obligation, a "should," in the color black. Mark everything you did that was a waste of time in red. Mark everything that brought you joy in blue, and everything that contributed to your growth in green. Mark everything you did to express yourself creatively in yellow. Flip through the book and see which colors dominate.

Were you satisfied with the results? How do you want this next year to look? What can you do about it? What *will* you do about it?

And the Brain Grows On

Contrary to popular belief, the struggle to balance uptime and downtime isn't completely the invention of a modern society that has turned us all into stimulus junkies. Stimulation is necessary for growth. Dr. Marian Cleeves Diamond says that in order to grow, develop, and maintain its organization, the brain needs constant challenge and stimulation. Stimulation is a critical factor in our survival. Just as we have been instinctually programmed to procreate, care for our young, find food and shelter, we have been instinctually programmed to crave stimulus.

The brain is designed to respond to stimulation and will grow in capacity as long as the environment is interesting and challenging. In a sense, the brain is a malleable organ, designed to expand its powers to meet the demands we place on it. For example, the part of the brain devoted to speech becomes larger and more developed in people who grow up speaking two or more languages fluently.

Scientific experiments have confirmed that changes in experience actually change the physiology of the brain. The brain shrinks or expands in response to stimulation or lack of it. At the University of California, Berkeley, Dr. Marian Cleeves Diamond has proved that, contrary to popular belief, the brain does not stop growing and lose cells with old age.

"We used to think that old dogs couldn't learn new tricks," she says, "but we can learn at any age. It just may take a little longer when we get older." When the brain cells stop being stimulated, the connections between the cells—the communicative dendrites—can deteriorate. Diamond found that when laboratory animals were deprived of adequate stimulation, their brain cortexes shrank, and conversely, when they were stimulated with social activity and toys, their brains grew.

"With our rats, if we have the same toys in the enriched environment for weeks on end, at first the brain grows with stimulation, but then they get bored with the toys and then the brain decreases its dimensions. So it's important to have new challenges," Dr. Diamond explains.

These and subsequent experiments proved that the structure of the brain changes based on input. This means that you can actually increase your creative abilities and intelligence by how you live your life; how much you stimulate your brain by incorporating new experiences into your life. So no matter what you've done up until this very moment, you can become smarter, more creative—and as a result, more fulfilled.

To keep adapting to a changing world, the brain constantly adjusts its circuitry and cell structure. We have a biological need to stay stimulated for survival, but too much of a good thing can be harmful.

As it grows and develops, the human brain becomes increasingly competent at receiving, decoding, and analyzing a complicated stream of information. During maturation, the capacity to discover and understand new things increases, as does the appetite and need for more stimulation.

The need for increasingly strong stimuli varies from person to person and from time to time during an individual's life. Some people thrive on the thrill of skydiving or white-water rafting; others need less stimulation. Having a cup of coffee, taking a nap, changing the level of lighting in a room, working with the radio on, drinking a glass of wine—all are examples of ways we increase or decrease our level of stimuli. We all have an optimum level of stimulus, yet finding that ever-changing balance is a continual process of fine-tuning. Finding the balance instead of being swept away by Lifespeed is key to living your life out loud.

Remember how as a child you could spend the better part of a summer afternoon fascinated by watching a ladybug or carefully writing the letters of the alphabet? Just think about how quickly you would become bored doing those things today.

We human creatures have an extremely low threshold for boredom and will naturally create stimulis. During psychological experiments, when people are deprived of stimulus, they rapidly lose the ability to concentrate, become disorganized, and their coordination and intellectual ability decline. When put into sensory deprivation, people try to seek stimulation by moving around or making sounds. Some people even begin to create their own worlds, complete with visual and auditory hallucinations. For centuries, a common form of torture and punishment has been the isolation of prisoners in dark, barren cells. It doesn't take long to break even the hardiest of individuals when all stimulus is removed from one's environment.

Paradoxically, the disorienting impact of sensory deprivation can also be beneficial. Sensory isolation has been used for relaxation and gaining deeper insights. For thousands of years, meditative techniques have been used to eliminate external distractions and achieve inner peace, tranquility, and expanded awareness.

One of the most brilliant leaders of the twentieth century, Mahatma Gandhi, regularly meditated for twenty-four hours at a stretch once a week and included shorter daily practice, too. Ray Kroc, founder of McDonald's, installed at hamburger headquarters in Oak Brook, Illinois, a tank with a seven-hundred-gallon waterbed, where he and his aides could steal some peace and quiet from the hectic pace of their hamburger empire.

The point is that you need to create a personal rhythm to balance stimulation and relaxation—one that you control. Gaining control over this balance is the first step in honoring yourself, and the foundation upon which you can design a more joyful, creatively expressive life.

EXERCISE

Write down three activities you wish you had more time to pursue. Along-side each, write down how much time each week you want to spend at this activity. Be Bold. This is your life!

Take out your pocketplanner or calendar and schedule those activities every week for the next three months. By spending this time with your favorite activities you will have begun a wonderful new habit of making the things you *really* enjoy doing a priority. What a concept!

Be a Creative Change Artist

Creative change comes from your willingness to incorporate new elements or activities into your life that will enhance it. It is the greatest way you can honor yourself, by being flexible and receptive enough to experiment with new ways of taking care of yourself. The suggestions that follow will help you tame the Lifespeed demon. Try the ones that appeal to you. And try a few that **don't** appeal to you—remember, we're going for flexibility here! You will be surprised how wonderful it feels to stretch beyond your comfort zone; to jump out of your rut and become a creative change artist.

1. **Set aside one afternoon each week with absolutely no plans.** Be spontaneous with the time; go with the flow. See how wonderful it feels.
2. **Learn to pause.** Taking mini breaks throughout the day is refreshing and reenergizing. Every hour or so, take ten minutes to refuel. Studies in peak performance have shown that people perform best when they can take a break from their work or routine every sixty to ninety minutes. Walk outside, sit quitely with your eyes closed (phone turned off), put on some music and stretch. Incorporate small, pause rituals into your daily

routine. For example: Write a poem each night before going to bed, say grace before or after meals, spend twenty minutes or more listening to music or sketching (even if you can't draw a straight line!)

3. **Meet stress head-on.** Develop your own special strategy for coping with stress. Meditation, self-hypnosis, relaxation techniques, getting out into nature, and exercise are all excellent ways to reduce the effects of stress on your life. Remind yourself that there is time for everything. When feeling stressed about deadlines and workloads, repeat this affirmation to yourself: *"I have all the time I need to do what I need to do."* Write it on a card and post it where you will see it as a constant reminder. It will calm you down and help you refocus on what you can do.

4. **Practice what author and spiritual teacher Eknath Eswaran, calls "one-pointed attention,"—focusing on one thing at a time, in mind and in action.** This means not watching television or reading while you eat, not putting on makeup while driving to work. Strange as it may sound, this takes incredible self-discipline and practice, especially if you are the superefficient type, priding yourself on how much you accomplish every day.

Eknath teaches that by slowing down and developing a one-pointed mind:

Your senses will be keener, your emotions more stable, your intellect more lucid, your sensitivity to the needs of others heightened . . . you won't forget things because your mind is engaged. You won't become mentally fatigued, for you are conserving your powers . . . and perhaps most precious of all, you will not ignore the distress or joy of others, because in looking into their eyes you will be looking truly into their hearts.

This approach is the essence of being present and in the moment.

5. **Arrange your environment to provide sanctuary from the outside world.** Don't answer the phone during mealtime and don't sleep with your head next to a telephone; or at least turn phones off at bedtime to avoid interruptions.

6. **Every morning, as soon as you awaken, ask yourself, "How do I want to pace my day?** How do I want the quality of my time to feel today?" Being conscious of what pace you want each day is the first step toward achieving it.

7. **Value your time—don't over schedule yourself.** You are in charge of your time and the pace of your life. Some Lifespeed addicts have learned to control their impulse to cram every minute of the day with an activity or obligation by scheduling in time for themselves to play, study, rest, or reflect—every day. Blocking out time slots will keep you from being overbooked and harried. Schedule daily playtime and contemplative time into your life. Make appointments with yourself *first*, then schedule other people and tasks.

8. **Exercise is a key to creativity.** Joan Price sums it up beautifully: "As good as your mind is, it's not at its best unless you've got the circulation going, the oxygen flowing, the blood flowing. Exercise feeds your brain, not just your muscles and your heart. If you take time for exercise it will give you back more time than it takes. If you take an hour for exercise, you haven't lost an hour in that day because you're going to get at least an hour more (maybe two or three) of really productive time where you are at high energy . . . your brain is working the best it can . . . your body feels good . . . you're motivated, you're relaxed and invigorated at the same time. There aren't too many fixes that can do that for you. Coffee doesn't. Sugar doesn't. Exercise does."

9. **Prepare a first-aid kit for the emotions and take the time to use it.** Read treasured correspondence from friends and loved ones, look at photographs that make you smile, play a favorite piece of music, reread quotes

or poems that inspire you. For years, Padi carried with her a letter from her father, written to her as she was getting ready to open her advertising agency at the age of twenty-seven. It was a letter of encouragement and has been read many times when she needed a love vitamin. The letter always boosts her confidence and makes her smile. Just by smiling, you change the chemistry in your brain to produce enzymes that actually make you feel better. That's why the "fake it till you make it" adage works—even by forcing a laugh or smile, you'll actually start feeling better.

10. **Take a close look at your social life and the people with whom you spend nonworking hours.** Are you maintaining relationships that no longer nurture you? Are you spending time with people with whom you share history but little else? Are you saying "Yes" when you should be saying "No, thank you"? If so, then it's time to retire some relationships.

    You know it's time to rethink a relationship when any of the following feelings come up: We don't have much in common anymore and there's not much to say to each other. This relationship doesn't feel mutually satisfying (i.e., I'm always on the giving end). I don't enjoy being around this person anymore; I notice after being with this person that I feel worse in some way (i.e., irritated, annoyed, depressed, low energy).

    Life is too short to spend your precious time with people who are toxic to your self-esteem, or don't contribute in some positive way to your life.

Sign seen on a retreat center bulletin board: "Things to do Today: Inhale, Exhale, Inhale, Exhale, etc."

11. **Make a commitment to yourself to start acting less like a human *doing* and *more* like a human *being!*** Practice being nonproductive, staring into space, listening quietly to your environment with closed eyes. Pay attention to the rate of your breathing. Read poetry. Give yourself permission to hang out!

Now that Salli is a grandmother, she spends a lot of time with her grandson "hanging out." When they are together, he gets her full attention, and she is learning to relax and rediscover the joy of just being. One afternoon she watched as Miles Dylan spent ten minutes with the sunlight on the wood floor. As he slowly turned, the patterns of sunlight shifted, sometimes disappearing to mysteriously reappear the next moment. By slowing down and focusing her attention, Salli has begun to rediscover the magic of being in the moment.

12. **Keep your 10% priority list handy, posted inside the cover of your appointment book and refer to it when making plans.** And keep a copy where you'll see it first thing in the morning.

13. **Just say no.** Practice under-scheduling yourself for a change. Instead of accepting every social invitation or volunteer/work assignment that comes along, start saying "No, thank you" more often. The more time you free up, the more time you'll have to pursue your creative endeavors, and then you'll have the perfect excuse: I'm working on a new (fill in the blank): painting, symphony, short story, film, recipe, solar irrigation system, or whatever.

14. **Do you really have to do it all?** If you find that you're doing too much, you may be able to slow down by spreading the work load more evenly among your family members or co-workers. If you can afford it, why not hire some help to free you from the more mundane chores and time-consuming tasks? Perhaps you could

EXERCISE

Make a list of all the things you love to do. Keep it where you can see it regularly as a reminder, and make sure you treat yourself to at least one item on your list *daily!*

trade for the help you need in return for tasks you enjoy, such as errands for cooking, house cleaning for baby-sitting, car washing for weed pulling.

It's important not to run on the fast track, but on *your* track. Pretend you have only six months to live, and make three lists; the things you *have* to do, *want* to do, and neither have to do nor want to do. Then, for the rest of your life, forget everything on the third list."

—ROBERT ELIOT, *professor of cardiology*

Making small, creative changes can make a big difference in your quality of life. By taming the Lifespeed Demon, you will have conquered one more joy crusher as you begin to make room for the activities that allow your creative juices to flow again.

12

Say No to Consumerism

With money in your pocket, you are wise and you are handsome and you sing well, too.

—YIDDISH PROVERB

I've got all the money I'll ever need, just so long as I die by four o'clock.

—HENNY YOUNGMAN

What exactly is money? A magic potion. A malevolent poison. A gift. A curse. A joy. A pain. A wonder. A worry. The root of all evil. The source of all happiness. Heaven and hell. Love and hate. Good and evil. Merriment and misery. Invention and abstraction. A state of mind, an attitude; a relationship between all things. According to economists, money is part of a system of relative pricing and an accounting store of value. According to many, it's sexy and slippery and hard to keep. According to some it's the very best thing in the world.

There is a lot of heartache in America surrounding money. Approximately 90% of all crimes are committed because of it, and according to the American Bar Association, 89% of all divorces are related to money problems. Even the golden years have become tarnished, as only one in twenty can look to retirement without family or other assistance.

In this chapter we will look at the philosophical underpinnings of our relationship with money, how the Gross National Product fuels a system based on a never-ending model of consumption and how consumerism robs us of our real wealth. We will look at how our monetary assets represent only a small portion of our real assets and see that by living more simply we can begin to come to grips with our addiction to things. The more unencumbered we become, the clearer our choices and the more in touch we become with who we are and our unlimited creative possibilities.

The GNP and Consumerism

All humans need to express themselves, yet most of us have severely narrowed our options to what money can buy. Instead of dancing, building a sand castle, flying a kite, growing a garden, reading a book, joining a choir, forming a rap group, or constructing a collage or a poem, we choose instead to express ourselves through the goodies we select, by the possessions we arrange about us. In a world where so many feel so powerless, where the illusion of expression-through-purchase is so readily accepted, isn't it inevitable that consuming has become the creative expression of choice?

Everyone needs an outlet.
—Billboard advertising factory outlet stores seen on Highway 80,
west of Sacramento, California

For many, the way they dress or decorate their homes or choose the car they drive becomes their *only* creative expression. We are not suggesting that there is anything wrong with dressing with care or living in an aesthetically pleasing environment. When these activities become a primary source of validation, however, they increasingly become pale reflections of your deeper creative expression. By paying too much attention to the stage set and the costumes, the play itself often becomes stilted and lacking in dimension.

If we are to take control of our money, rather than letting money take control of us, it's helpful to understand the role the GNP plays in our lives. Theoretically, the GNP, or gross national product, is a report card designed to measure our standard of living. The GNP has become the indicator of the quality of our lives, a shorthand for the well-being of our nation. It drives growth, measures economic progress, and is used as a basis for tax revenues. It is a measurement of the total output of goods and services in the United States, and it has also become the international standard for ranking countries from poor to rich.

Simply put, the GNP is based on money changing hands; it measures cash flow only. It does not measure *real* value. If we sell our home, it's counted in the GNP. If we have a bike wreck and end up in the hospital, that cost is also added to the GNP. The nation makes money from the Los Angeles earthquake, as individuals and merchants repair and replace all that was damaged. The repairing after floods in Mississippi, cleaning up Alaskan oil spills, putting one's parents in a convalescent home—all increase the GNP. In other words, America's GNP would indicate progress and a higher quality of life if we logged all of the rain forest in the Northwest—simply because money has changed hands.

The Exxon Valdez disaster in Alaska; the radioactive disaster zone of Hanford, Washington; the proliferation of every form of cancer in our society—these are not the "price of progress." They are the price of profit, the price of corporate thinking about human values, the price of a materialism so corrosive that it can rupture an oil tanker's hull, or a nuclear reactor's containment vessel.

—RABBI ALEXANDER M. SCHINDLER

True Wealth

How does the GNP affect your joy and creativity? When money is used as the prime indicator of social welfare, it tragically distorts the meaning of true wealth. True wealth is good health, loving relationships, being connected with the earth and self-expression. We know in our hearts that these are the values that matter. Wealth is not merely savings and investments, imports and exports; these are abstractions. **Net worth does not equal self-worth.** As a country, our real wealth is our natural resources and the skills and insights of our people. The pursuit of money is not the root of all evil, but neither is it the source of fulfillment, happiness, a better world, or anything else that we humans hold so dear.

The true indicator of a society's well-being is not GNP, but GNH—gross national happiness.

—KING OF BHUTAN

As Norman Lear so eloquently stated in the *Washington Post*: "The truth is, however, that living by the numbers is not a happy way to live one's life. Let's face it, we are not a nation enjoying its material success. And it should be obvious by now that a higher GNP, a faster computer chip, and interactive television with 500 channels are not going to address the hole in America's heart, a direct result of the spiritual poverty of our time."

Does Money Make You Happy?

All my possessions for a moment of time.

—QUEEN ELIZABETH I, *with her dying breath, 1603*

As a culture, we have been conditioned to equate money with happiness, yet among the people we interviewed for this book or have counseled and worked with over the years, those who have a lot of money do not seem any happier or more secure than those without much money.

According to Brad Edmondson in the July/August 1991 *Utne Reader*, "Fewer than 5% of Americans earning less than $15,000 per year say they have achieved the American Dream. Just 6% of those earning more than $50,000 per year say they have." Yet many young people still hope that more money will make them happier. The July/August 1992 issue of *Psychology*

Today reported that in 1970, 39% of students entering college said "becoming well off financially" was an important life goal. In 1991, that rose to 74%.

Money can't buy you happiness, but it *can* buy you possessions. And there is definitely a correlation between the income you make and the amount of possessions you acquire. The more income you earn, the more you spend. And the expectation is that you will always want more. Many people are not content to spend all they make—they spend more than they make. Seemingly unable or unwilling to curb their consuming, they must pay for this habit on credit. The more in debt they are, the more trapped they feel, and the more they need to substitute "things" for peace of mind. It's so easy to get out of balance, to discover yourself in a hopeless maze of mortgages and credit card debts, not really enjoying your life anymore, yet helpless to navigate your way out.

> **S**een on a shopping bag in San Francisco: "See it. Like it.
> Buy it."

Kate Bishop, who until recently designed silk gowns for women who "didn't want to discuss babies or bills over dinner," remembers what her priorities were like before she and her family took a year off to reestablish what was important in their lives:

> I was caught up in the rat race. For example, I was working too hard, so instead of going someplace where I could buy food at a reasonable price and stock up in advance, I didn't have time to make that shopping trip. So I would go down to the local convenience store at the bottom of the hill where everything is expensive and buy a few things at a time. At the end of the month we would have a big bill at the store and didn't feel very good about our family scene.

When you are caught up in this kind of cycle it's hard to get out. As with Kate, the more you work, the more you feel you need; the more possessions you "deserve." You become part of a fiendish dance with a disturbing beat, acquire, produce,

produce, consume, consume, consume. The media is quick to remind: "You deserve a break today." "You only live once." "Shop till you drop." The bombardment of these messages is relentless. We would like to propose a New American Dance. A slower dance, one with a soft, steady beat with slogans like: "Do you really need it?" "I'm a consumer defector," "Connection, not consumerism," "Less is more," and "Just say no—to more stuff."

> **O**nly then when the last tree is cut, when the last river is poisoned, when the last fish is caught, only then you will know that one cannot eat money.
> —KENYAN FARMER

In America, the phrase "disposable income" is so commonly used that few question its oxymoronic nature. What we make and what we buy are fairly shoddy goods. What a manufacturer might call "designed obsolescence" is a standard practice in industry. 'Disposable' is the term we use for things that lack quality and durability. Getting in the habit of discarding means we never even get to appreciate our possessions. They have no patina. Since we don't treasure our possessions, it's fairly painless to discard them, which keeps the whole consumer process gyrating. Even when things are made well, we are encouraged to discard them as new and better models continually become available. It's interesting and revealing that while "consume" means to eat and drink, it also means to destroy, demolish, annihilate, burn, exhaust, corrode, devour, and use up.

> **T**he children's market was $75 billion dollars in 1990. Teens spent more time at the mall than anywhere other than school and home.

The Hidden Price of Consumerism

Putting aside what the production of so much stuff does to our planetary resources, let's look at what consumerism does to the consumer in a more personal way. There is no gentle way to say it, so here goes: **Every minute you work for more than you actually need, you are stealing time from the rest of your life.** As Henry David Thoreau said, "The price of anything is the amount of life you exchange for it." We only get so much time, and as yet no one has figured out how to buy more.

Joe Domingues and Vicki Robin make clear in their excellent book *Your Money or Your Life* the price most of us pay for obtaining the money necessary to feed our addiction to consumerism:

> Money is something we choose to trade our life energy for. This definition of money gives us significant information. Our life energy is more *real* in our actual experience than money. You could even say money *equals* our life energy. So while money has no intrinsic reality, our life energy does—at least to us. It's tangible, and it's finite. The key is remembering that *anything* you buy and don't use, *anything* you throw away, *anything* you consume and don't enjoy is money down the drain, wasting your life energy *and* wasting the finite resources of the planet.

Learning to live more contentedly with less income and less consumption of goods vastly outranks all other things we might choose to do to lessen our ecological impacts. Odd as it may seem, the simple act of consuming less is probably the most radical step you can personally take to save the Earth.
—ERNEST CALLENBACH, *Living Cheaply with Style*

The American model of abundant consumption—the standard for much of the world— is beginning to unravel. Although inevitable, given the increased awareness of the personal and planetary harm we have wrought, living with less is not going to be an easy shift. We are not a nation used to pulling in our belts; we are accustomed to quick fixes, ready-made formulas, and instant gratification. The country's economic problems are complex. Being a generous people, largely unaware of how deeply ingrained and unhealthy our *need* to consume is, we would like the whole world to join us on the throwaway, consumer bandwagon. The more the merrier. Clearly this model cannot work, and the more creative we can be about consuming less and putting money needs into perspective, the better off everyone will be.

I'd rather be a poor man in the center of heaven than a rich man in the corner of hell.
—Tattoo seen on a Fijian from the Island of Waya

As you begin to change your compulsive buying habits and free up more time for creativity, it's necessary to address some unmet and basic psychological needs such as security, appreciation, status, and relationships. Notice how you feel when you buy something and think about why buying has taken on such significance in your life. Ask some difficult questions: What aren't you getting in your life? Are you substituting "stuff" for yourself in important relationships?

What role does self-esteem play in consumerism? What happens to your self-esteem and sense of security when the bills come due, and what do you do about it? Why do the solutions to so many human problems appear to be found in buying things?

The consumer society fails to deliver on its promise of fulfillment through material comforts because human wants are insatiable, human needs are socially defined, and the real sources of personal happiness are elsewhere.
—ALAN DURNING, *How Much Is Enough?*

EXERCISE

Keep a record of the next ten purchases (other than groceries) you make. Record even the smallest ones.

Write next to these purchases how you felt immediately before and after buying them.

Write down the total cost of these ten purchases.

Figure out how many hours in work time it cost you to purchase the items.

Was it a good trade?

Write down the last five major purchases you have made. How did you feel about those purchases before and after buying them?

Did you pay cash or are you still paying for these purchases? If you are still paying, is it still worth it?

If you are addicted to smoking, you can see a hypnotist, join a group, wear a patch, smoke tobacco-free cigarettes, chew mints and gum or even your own fingernails. You will hopefully gets lots of support for trying to quit. If you are addicted to shopping, what can you do?

EXERCISE

1. Form an informal support group. Make the pool of people large enough so that you can always find someone available. Anytime you are about to plunk down some hard-earned cash for something you want and don't need, call up one of the people in your group and let them talk you out of it.

2. Borrow from friends. We counted ten canoes in the garages and back-yards of our friends. When we asked how often they used those canoes, the average answer was twice a year! If you want to go canoeing or camping or anything that isn't already an integral part of your life, check with friends first. You will receive benefits to both your bank account and sense of community.

EXERCISE

1. Every time you reach for plastic, checkbook, or cash, ask yourself if this is something you really need or if it just makes you feel good to buy it. As a reminder, place a note in your wallet by your credit cards that says "Why am I buying this?" Do this exercise for a week. Make it a habit.

2. Try leaving the house for a day without plastic and a checkbook. Bring ten dollars in your pocket to be used only in case of emergency. If this feels terrifying, think about why. Do it anyway.

3. Once you get in the habit of asking why you so quickly and so often are willing to part with your money, ask yourself if you really want to trade your time for this "stuff." Given the choice, would you really rather buy your grandchild a new toy or take him to the park? Would you rather watch the sunset every night for a week or work late so you can buy a new sweater?

Getting Unhooked from Consumerism

If you perceive you have a lot more than your share of goodies, are overwhelmed by the clutter in your closets, feel as if you live in the middle of an ongoing garage sale, yet continue to acquire more, you are in the throes of "shopaholism." Although not everyone is consumer crazed or feels the need to constantly upgrade their possessions, most Americans do spend an inordinate amount of time either shopping or fantasizing about things to buy. Most of us are shopaholics suffering from a collective and ongoing low-grade infection. And we don't even realize we are sick! The first step in shaking any addiction is to realize there is a problem and want to get well.

Here is a list of alternative things to consider when you feel down in the dumps, need a self-esteem booster shot, or a feeling of power and control over your life, times when you might normally cruise the mall. All of these ideas are meant to get you to experience life firsthand and to fully participate in the world around you. These alternatives to consumption feel good and don't cost anything. And there is no debt to pay later. And like any addiction, once free of it, your creativity will soar.

1. **Have a clothes swap.** At Salli's "Most Memorable Clothes Swap" she invited women who were approximately the same size to bring clothes they no longer wanted and would be happy to pass on to a special friend. About fifteen women showed up and had a wonderful time oohing and aahing over each other's treasures. Often, several women lusted after the same garment, so a spontaneous process evolved to make sure everyone left happy. Years later people still talk

about how great it was to add something "new-to-them" to their wardrobe and have so much fun in the process.

2. **Massage your own neck or shoulder or hands.** When Salli had a severely sore neck, a body worker suggested she warm some oil between her hands and massage her own neck every day. What a wonderful way to reconnect, to slow down and nurture yourself. Sometimes we shop when what we really need is a little T.L.C.

3. **Spend an afternoon with a child** (yours or someone else's) doing exactly what *they* want to do. Discover the joys of bowling, hopscotch, or video games.

4. **Go for a bike ride.** Borrow one, or pump up the tires on yours, and see the world from a new perspective.

5. **Have a tea party.** Use your best dishes, put on some good music, and invite a friend over.

6. **Bring some soup to a neighbor's house.** Padi and her husband make extra soup or stew on the weekend, and once a month bring a container over to their neighbors to share. The neighbors love the surprise and reciprocate when they can. Since they all have busy lifestyles, the treat is especially appreciated.

7. **Forgive someone.** Pick up that phone and offer your forgiveness. Letting go of an old hurt of resentment can free up energy to be more creative and at peace with yourself.

8. **Take a bubble bath, candles optional.** Really soak in the suds till your fingers wrinkle up.

9. **Sing in the car, or the shower, or the Met!**—at the top of your lungs.

10. **Clean out your closet.** You'll probably find things you forgot you even had and realize how much you do have that you probably don't use.

Money is neither good nor bad, magic potion nor malevolent poison. It is simply a tool. And you can abuse that tool, or use it merely to survive, or turn it into a tool for joy and creative expression. As Benjamin Franklin said, "Joy is not in things. It is in us." Once you consciously decide how much is enough for you, once you get clear about the trade-off you make whenever you make a purchase, you will free up tremendous amounts of creative energy. This is *not* a punitive exercise. The vision of being carried kicking and screaming out of Bloomingdale's is not what we are suggesting. For those who see the wisdom in breaking free—willingly to take the plunge into discovering how much is enough—the rewards are straightforward: Once free of consumer addiction, you will not only be able to tap deeper into your creative energy; you will feel saner, more in control, and able to enjoy the satisfaction that comes from contributing to the transformation of an economic system gone haywire.

What money can and cannot buy is the lesson of this Italian fable.

THE HAPPY MAN'S SHIRT

There was once a king who had an only son whom he loved more than anything else in the world. But the prince was unhappy, and no matter what the king did to cheer him up, he grew sadder day by day.

It seemed as if the poor youth was withering away from melancholy, though he could not explain what was wrong or what could be done about it. The king became quite desperate and issued a decree calling the most learned doctors, philosophers, and professors from all corners of the world to come to the palace to examine the prince. The wise ones withdrew to consult with each other after seeing the prince, and when they returned to the king they told him this: "Your Majesty, we have given much thought and study to this matter, and after consulting each other and the stars, here is what must be done. Find a happy man, a man who is happy through and through, and exchange your son's shirt for his."

The next day, the king sent his ambassadors to all parts of the world to find the happiest man. Each time one of the king's envoys thought they had found a truly happy man, it turned out he wanted for something else, or worried that he would lose his happiness! The ambassadors returned to the king without a shirt. Overcome with grief, the king decided to go hunting. He fired at a hare, but only wounded it, and off it scampered on three legs. The king ran after it, leaving his hunting party behind. Suddenly, he heard the sound of a man singing gaily. "Whoever sings like that surely sounds happy to me!" he exclaimed. Following the song, he came to an old vineyard, where he saw a young man pruning the vines as he sang.

"Good morning, Your Majesty," said the smiling youth.

"How would you like to come to the palace with me and be my friend?" asked the king.

"I do thank you," said the singer, "but I couldn't even consider it. I wouldn't even change places with the Pope. I'm content with where I am and what I have and want for nothing."

Finally, a happy man, thought the king. My son is saved! The king told the youth to wait and ran to get his retinue. "Come at once! My son is saved!" he shouted. He took them to the young man. "Dear lad," he began. "My son is dying, and only you can save him. I'll give you whatever you want, But I must ask you to give me . . ." The king grabbed him and began unbuttoning his jacket. All of a sudden he stopped, and his arms fell to his sides.

The happy man wore no shirt.

Say Yes to a
Simpler Lifestyle

The greatest wealth is to live content with little.

—PLATO

Simple living is a way of *being,* not a way of doing. It's about being true to yourself and honoring your deeper values. It's *not* about deprivation. Simple living is challenging, fulfilling, and extremely liberating. By simplifying your life, you have so much more control over the way you spend your time. You can be more flexible and more spontaneous. You can discover more peace, contentment, and tranquility.

The less complex your lifestyle, the more freedom, options, contentment, and creativity you make room for in your life. Living simply is not enforced frugality. It's a purposeful strategy that both reduces your consumption and lowers your expenses. Simple living is almost magical in that it gives you much more control over time and incredible flexibility. Few things are more freeing than a simplified lifestyle.

Kate Bishop, a fashion designer and mother of two, gained valuable perspective and insights about living simply when she took a year off to sail with her family.

On the boat we had no phone, no fax, no car, no utilities, and no one calling us up with a plan for how to spend our time. We became so much more aware and responsible for our actions on the boat. For instance, you have to bring all your own water on board, and therefore you consider carefully how you will use that water. There are no services on board, so if something breaks, you fix it yourself. The more electronic gadgets you have, the more things there are to break, so you learn to make sane decisions about what you need. Luxury items quickly become a pain.

I realized how happy I was on the boat. Before we left I would wake up in the middle of the night and start going over the bills in my head and the appointments that I had made and think about how was I ever going to manage to fulfill all the obligations I had set for myself. When we were cruising, I found myself waking up in the middle of the night and going up and sitting on deck and listening to the waves and looking at the moon and just enjoying being there. God, what a difference!

It's as if we're juggling too many balls. You start out juggling two easily, and then you find out you actually can handle a third without dropping them, and then you add a fourth and fifth, and pretty soon you're juggling six balls, and they're falling all over the place, and you're running and catching them up and getting them all in the air again, and it doesn't even occur to you that you don't need to be juggling six balls.

Keeping life simple and balanced is important to Mirium Redstone, a therapist who works exclusively with women in transition. "I love my work", Mirium says, "I choose to have only four or five clients at any given time so I have plenty of time for my daughter, who is five and is being home schooled, my husband, David, and for myself. And I am so glad to be able to be with myself. I don't have to make an appointment to be with myself. I know what I like to do, and part of what I enjoy is having lots of quiet time to pay attention to my own rhythms.

Mirium is very clear about balancing what's important in her life:

Our goal is to provide for our family and do community service, but not to amass a lot of money. David and I are tax resisters and do not support the idea that half of all federal tax monies should go to the military, so that's also a factor in our decision to earn less than we could. We do put money into socially responsible investments and try to make sure any company connected with an investment group reflects our values.

We have figured out how much we need to pay our bills and help provide our daughter with choices she might make, and that's plenty for us. We live very simply; dinner is rice and a salad, and whatever greens are growing in our garden. I do very little shopping; mainly ordering in bulk through our neighborhood food co-op. David and I go out once a week to a movie or dinner—it's a ritual we have shared since we had our daughter. I'm glad we have a roof over our head, and when it's rainy or cold outside we are dry and under blankets, and our bellies are not hungry. I am thrilled every day just for that. I feel so fortunate.

Mirium could work five days a week and see twenty clients a week. She would have a lot more money, but she wouldn't have the things she *really* wants.

Miller Phoenix was a district manager for a jewelry store chain until her health made her take a good look at the price she was paying for "success."

I had a large territory. I would go to the stores and motivate people and teach them how to merchandise and hire and fire managers. My health went bad, and I got cancer for the second time. I thought, "Nope, the money's not worth it. I have choices over my health." I changed my work and chose a simpler lifestyle. I made a lot of money. I was successful, and I made a choice to get out. I didn't want to keep working for things. Things are temporary.

Now I run a fine art co-op gallery where I can really be

myself and be in business. I'm a painter and a sculptor. Right now I'm into my garbage art, taking recyclable things and making them into objects. Junk that people are throwing out I eventually weld or put into another form and it becomes a sculpture.

Since I changed my priorities, I have not been ill with cancers, and I've been a lot happier. Stuff isn't that important. My life is a lot less complicated. Money and clothes and all the things that people work toward are superfluous to me. We can either just be and enjoy the moment of being, or we can work like crazy for stuff. A bigger house, a better car, more clothes, newer shoes.

I like to eat good food, I like good friends, I like to be warm. I like to be able to take time to enjoy. You get the best clothes at the thrift stores. I redye or remake things. You have to work extra hours to shop at department stores. We don't buy new cars. We bought our cabin for a very reasonable price, and we have real low payments. We fixed it up on our own, so it's not fancy but it's very livable. We just don't do middle-class American things. We don't eat out because we eat better at home. Most of our money is spent taking care of our animals and eating good food and buying wood for the winter. Very simple.

Life itself is the proper binge.
—JULIA CHILD

The more complex your lifestyle, the more time and money needed to maintain and worry about it, protect and insure it.

EXERCISE

Write down all the stuff in one room of your house. Everything, including the contents of every drawer and closet. You probably will have writer's cramp after a half hour!

EXERCISE

Keep a possessions' maintenance log for a month—note how much time and money you spend on fixing, replacing, and caring for your stuff. Include dry cleaning, car repairs, etc. in your log.

Clean your closets! Go on a de-accumulation binge. Get into a give-away frenzy. Anything you haven't worn in a year can probably go. Friends, relatives, or charities like Good Will Industries and the Salvation Army will really appreciate your cast-offs, and you'll have the pleasure of knowing someone who really needs these items is using them.

Time is our most precious personal resource and the single most effective way to have more of it is to live more simply. By learning to conserve your resources and reduce the amount of things you purchase, you will not need to work as hard to create a sustainable income, and you will have more time for creative expression. The act of becoming more resourceful is in itself a creative act that will lead to more creativity. As you begin to clear away some of the material clutter in your life, you uncover your *truly* valuable resources and reap the benefits of living more simply.

Getting a Handle on Your Money

Although we laugh at the joke about not having money when we still have all those blank checks left, many of us actually do operate our finances along similar lines. You are not alone!

In order to live more simply, decide what is necessary to spend money on in your life and what you are spending money on that is a habit you no longer want. You really need a plan if you want to change your way of thinking about money. The idea is to live your values, not to exist in a state of deprivation, and that means having a clear picture of your finances. Most of us really don't have a clue as to how much money we spend on what. We recommend the following exercise suggested by Amy Dacyczyn, the publisher of *The Tightwad Gazette,* to help you get clear about where your money goes.

EXERCISE

The most elementary exercise for any aspiring tightwad is to record spending habits for a period of three months. Write down EVERYTHING, from the mortgage payment to the candy bar at the checkout counter.

All of your expenses will be one of two types. Essential and optional. Essential expenses are things that you absolutely cannot cut. Optional expenses are nonessential. For example, your phone bill has a minimum service charge that you must pay to have telephone service and a breakdown for long-distance calls. The ten-dollar call to your mother was optional. Your food bill contains items necessary for basic nutrition and nonnutritious items like coffee, candy, and soda, which are optional.

No one but you can say exactly where the line between essential and optional expenses falls. That depends on YOUR value system. The point is to understand how much you *really* have left over to play with.

If you take home $20,000 per year, and of that, $15,000 is already allocated for essential expenses, the $5,000 remaining is what you have left for optional expenses. In that light, making a small adjustment to save $1,000 a year makes more sense. As you further fine-tune your spending, you may realize that only $12,000 of your take-home is actually essential and you have even more room for savings.

By tracking your spending in this way, for the first time you will have a truly clear picture of where your best options for cutbacks are. It will also give you a valuable gauge for comparison as you gain success at managing your money.

Once you understand where your money goes, you will be equipped to formulate a financial plan and set some goals for gaining control over your money. The above exercise will take time and commitment to master—after all, you have probably spent years unconsciously letting money fly out of your pocket.

We know someone who did this exercise and discovered, much to her shock, that she was spending about $75 each month on café lattes! Another friend was embarrassed to discover that his family of four had consumed nine take-out Chinese dinners one month, totaling $300—enough to feed a peasant family of four in China for a year! Enough for him to not have to work overtime anymore. You, too, will be amazed at where your money goes when you track it. Getting in the habit of recording every penny you spend is admittedly a challenge. Make it fun. Reward yourself with something that money can't buy—such as time with friends, a walk in a park, a nap, listening to or playing music, an afternoon at your local library.

EXERCISE

Make a budget. Now that you know where your money goes, ask yourself if you want to, or can afford to, continue spending it in the way you do. You don't need to track it for a year; once you have kept track for a few months, you will have a pretty good idea of the categories needed to make your customized budget. A budget is a reminder, a plan for how you have chosen to allocate your monetary resources. Look upon your budget with fondness, for it can help set you free. A budget is not like a diet. Once you view it as a blueprint for freedom, you will grow to love your parameters. By determining how much money you need, you can realistically begin to create the life you want.

Frugality

Americans used to regard thrift as a virtue. The time-honored skills of making do, using up, repairing, trading, and bartering are an important part of our heritage. Our present disposable culture is a relatively new phenomenon, and it's not healthy for the earth. According to Robert Muller, former assistant secretary general to the United Nations, "The single most important thing any of us can do for the planet is a return to frugality."

If frugality is a new concept for you, be prepared for initial awkwardness as you look at your life in a brand-new way. You are a pioneer, pushing past the old boundaries into a new frontier as you discover what is essential for your life. Your friends and family members might not support you at first. Remember, to a greater or lesser degree, almost everyone in our culture overconsumes.

There is a strong movement of people who are embracing frugality. Many of them read the informative and fun newsletter *The Tightwad Gazette*, which helps you cut pennies in ways you never dreamed of. Publisher Amy Dacyczyn, known affectionately as the "frugal zealot," practices penny pinching because: "By learning how to optimize my time and resources I can create a tax-free income. I can elevate the standard of living of our family without working more hours outside the home."

Authors of the bestselling book *Your Money or Your Life,* Joe Domingues and Vicki Robin describe frugality as "honoring and valuing your most precious resource—your life energy. Shopping smart, saving money, following the adage use it up, make it do, do without, wear it out isn't about deprivation; it's about loving yourself and your life so much that you wouldn't think of wasting a second."

Having better, bigger seems to be part of the human condition. Resisting our impulse for more, and appreciating what we have, can be a lifelong lesson. We share this ancient Japanese parable with you, as it so simply expresses this truth.

Voluntary Simplicity

Voluntary simplicity is usually associated with saints, monks, the counterculture, dropouts, and hippies. While voluntary simplicity may appeal to some people in these groups, it is actually a meaningful and practical way of life for a cross section of the population. In fact, according to Trends Research Institute in New York, voluntary simplicity was one of the top ten trends of 1994.

THE STONECUTTER

There was once a poor stonecutter who bemoaned his life and wished he could be a rich man. A magic genie appeared to him and granted him his wish. The stonecutter found he had everything money could buy. Soon after, on a very hot day, the man noticed how powerful the sun was. "I wish I were the sun!" he exclaimed.

The genie granted him his second wish and the man delighted in shining upon the earth in his luminous brilliance. But then some clouds appeared and covered him up. "They are stronger than me!" he shouted, and he wished he could become a cloud. This wish, too, was granted. The man rained all over the earth and was thrilled in his power to wash everything away.

Then he noticed that the mountain didn't wash away—it was unmovable. "The mountain is stronger than me!" he cried out, and he wished to be the mountain. Once again, his wish was granted, and he became the mountain. For a while he rejoiced in being eternal and unchanging, until one day he noticed someone chipping away at his feet. It was a stonecutter, removing great blocks from the mountain. "How can this be?" the man shouted. "I am the mountain, but that man is stronger than me. I wish I were him!" So his fifth wish was granted, and the stonecutter found himself back at the beginning, except that now he was content with his lot.

Voluntary simplicity is not just a passing trend, however. It is a powerful concept emphasizing inner riches and material simplicity. It is a spiritually based way of life that addresses many social issues, such as loss of community, bureaucratic burden, global alienation, and ecological overload.

It is often mistakenly assumed that simple livers are childlike persons who are merely justifying their involuntary poverty or are caught up in some irresponsbile fad. Yet living simply has nothing to do with how much or how little money you make. Rather it's a liberating philosophy of nonattachment to both money and possessions, a philosophy that nurtures and develops resourcefulness.

An important aspect of voluntary simplicity is commitment

to taking responsibility for your actions. According to Richard Gregg, the first to write about American voluntary simplicity, in the mid 1930s, voluntary simplicity "means singleness of purpose, sincerity and honesty within, as well as avoidance of exterior clutter . . . a partial restraint in some directions, in order to secure greater abundance of life in other directions."

In their book *Simple Living Investments*, Michael Phillips and Catherine Campbell define simple living as: "an artful weave of care for the environment, attentiveness to one's individual contribution to the community, a concern for personal humility, and a love of the beautiful, the erotic, and the spontaneous. Simple living today is joyful, bright, poetic, and mentally robust."

Infoglut

Our obsession with numbers, the quantifiable, the immediate, has cost us our connection with that place in each of us that honors the unquantifiable and eternal—our capacity for awe, wonder and mystery; that place where acts of faith in a process larger than ourselves prove ultimately satisfying in the fullness of time.

—NORMAN LEAR, *The Washington Post,* June 1993

Part of living simply includes managing information. It is no wonder that information overload—infoglut—overwhelms us. Within eight years, half of the technical knowledge we now possess will have been replaced. It has been estimated that the amount of information available doubles every five years. Every year, over one thousand new words are added to the Oxford English Dictionary. More than eleven thousand magazines are published in the United States; over one thousand books are published daily worldwide.

Every day, the average American is exposed to more than fifteen hundred advertising messages via billboards, radio, television, newspapers, direct mail, signs, bumper stickers, on-hold phone commercials, shopping mall kiosks, and imprinted merchandise. Many cable television subscribers receive up to one hundred and forty channels, and digital video compression technology turns fifty-channel systems into five hundred-channel behemoth monsters. Consider this: A viewer who spends five seconds surfing each channel would need almost forty-two minutes just to see what's available. By then, most of the programs will have changed!

> Information itself does not enlighten. We cannot clarify what is mis-information, dis-information, or propaganda in this media-dominated "spin-doctored" environment. Focusing on mere information has led to overload of ever-less-meaningful billions of bits of fragmented raw data and sound bites, rather than the search for meaningful new patterns of knowledge.
> —HAZEL HENDERSON, *Paradigms in Progress: Life Beyond Economics*

Infoglut is a major contributor to Lifespeed—the shrinkage of our precious time due to external factors that detract and distract from the quality of our life. With the growing jungle of data, faxes, phone messages, all-day news broadcasts, and the ever-quickening pace of change, the pressure to be "up" on everything is intense. And needing to be up on everything is a deterrent to living a simple lifestyle.

In order to experience more joy in your life, you need time to savor the present moment and get out from the constant rush mode. You need more pauses in each day, more open space for your mind to wander, your heart to feel, your creativity to blossom. You need less extraneous information to suck up every spare moment of your time.

There is nothing intrinsically wrong with the desire for information. In our fast-changing world, it is important to keep abreast of matters that impact our lives, economically, socially, politically, professionally. It is the *extent* to which we submerge ourselves in this constant flow of data, becoming victims to it rather than taking control of it, that is the problem.

The information explosion has brought with it powerful messages that society has embraced: Knowledge is power; the more you know, the higher you'll go. Many of us have allowed ourselves to become addicted to information because we have accepted these myths without questioning their validity.

It's a vicious cycle. Like a dog chasing its tail, you can never catch up or stay on top of everything you think you should know about. Each time you get closer to the bottom of the pile, another tidal wave of information threatens to drown you. It is simply impossible to keep up with it all, and trying to do so is not only unhealthy, it can blow out your creative fuses.

The more bits of data you collect and distract yourself with, the less time you leave for integrating the data and mentally massaging it. The only way you can productively and creatively use the information you gather is to allow incubation time to process it. Making the information relevant and useful comes from letting it rattle around in a mind that takes time out and has the space to wander and make new, meaningful connections from all the data. The more time you spend harvesting information, the less time you have to let it stew and brew into your own knowledge base and creative expression.

Jeff Davidson, author of *Breathing Space*, says that more information is generated in a day than you could comfortably ingest for the rest of your life. He explains: "Too much information violates our senses and even becomes harmful. As you receive more information you experience stress, anxiety, and even helplessness . . . the feeling of no breathing space can quickly pervade all aspects of your life, diminish your happiness, and eliminate any *joie de vivre*."

There's an increasingly insidious amount of information that attacks us, like telemarketers at dinnertime, compounding our stress and anxiety. Think about how, increasingly, you combine information-gathering with other activities. How often have you seen couples dining out while each reads a section of the newspaper throughout the meal? Neither reading nor eating nor socializing gets the attention it deserves, nor does it provide true enjoyment, because the attention is splintered.

By combining information gathering with other activities, we are not being fully present with either task; we are not practicing one-pointed attention. The reason so many people complain that their reading retention or memory is poor may be because no one can give full attention to learning or listening when it's combined with another activity.

Infogluttony also has another frightening side effect. It shrinks the time you have to live your life. We lament having no time for hobbies, being with friends and family, taking a walk. Americans spend 40% less time with their children today than they did in 1965. It is estimated that the average couple spends under five minutes a day in meaningful conversation.

Yet, according to Simmons Market Research Bureau, New York, the average American spends thirty-seven minutes daily reading the newspaper. This means that in a seventy-five-year lifetime, (subtracting the first fifteen years as non-newspaper reading time) the typical American spends 13,505 hours or 337 work weeks or 168 two-week vacations reading the newspaper during their lifetime. This translates to nearly two and a half years of waking-hour life. Since Americans start watching television at a very young age, we spend more than eight years of our lives watching television.

Imagine: If you reduced your news-gathering time to just ten minutes daily, you could use the remaining time to learn a new language, write in your journal, try a new recipe, practice yoga, take up watercolors, take piano lessons, soak in a bubble bath, play with your children, read some great fiction . . . or whatever *you* would do if you were given twenty-seven minutes more a day!

When you consider that only about 13% of the newspaper is devoted to hard news, 24% devoted to soft news (feature stories, crime, scandals, columnists, etc.) and a whopping 73%

EXERCISE

Not enough time to relax, recharge your creative batteries, play? Figure out how much time you spend daily gathering information. Include reading the newspaper, television watching, time on the telephone, reading professional journals and news magazines. Track your information gathering habits for a week in each category and notice where your time goes. You'll be able to determine quickly if you need to go on an info diet in any of the categories.

to advertising, it may be easier to decide if you want to spend two and a half entire years of your life devoted to reading the daily paper thoroughly.

Now we're not criticizing the average American, or anyone who spends time gathering information—if that's really what they want to be doing. However, out of habit, many of us unknowingly waste precious hours collecting data we don't really need or want, thereby throwing away years we could have employed more pleasantly. Gathering some information is a necessary part of living in our society—but so much of the information we gather, if carefully analyzed, contributes nothing of real value to our lives or our understanding of the world. Instead of reading every newspaper article, try skimming headlines of the less important stories. Reading every other issue of a magazine you subscribe to can keep you up to date because of the repetition factor. It's time to stop feeling guilty about not reading everything and to start reading only what you need and want.

> The average American child sees 6,000 hours of television before entering kindergarten at age five. This has taken the place of what would have been the child's ordinary imaginative play. You see, play is the critical way in which the brain develops in the first seven years and up till age eleven. . . . So, television cripples development of intelligence. People say that it gives so much information, but the child needs visual information of that sort like a hole in the head. Information is not what nature's after—she's after ability. The capacity to create imagery is the way by which all learning takes place in the first eleven years.
>
> —JOSEPH CHILTON PEARCE on *A World of Ideas with Bill Moyers*

Avoid Becoming a Roadkill on the Information Superhighway

How can you stop being victimized by infoglut? How can you simplify your life and avoid becoming roadkill on the information superhighway? It takes some weaning and self-discipline, but the rewards of letting go and not having to know everything about everything are numerous. More time for creative endeavors, less stress, and a greater sense of well-being are some of the benefits to be gained when you consciously choose where, when, and how to focus your attention. Here are some suggestions:

1. Create your own personal table of contents. Make a list by subject matter of everything you *really* want to keep up with. Keep it handy where you'll see it regularly as a reminder of what is really important in your life. Put this on your desk, bathroom mirror, or appointment book to keep yourself focused on your information priorities. We keep several files of information that interest us and clip and save specifically for those files. Sometimes we'll just skim a magazine, tear out the articles we want to read, and throw the rest of the magazine in the recycling pile so we won't be tempted to read the other stuff *just because it's there*. If skimming is difficult for you, learning how to speed-read is another efficient way to reduce the time spent consuming information.

Do you really want to spend eight months of your life opening junk mail? According to Dan Sperling in "Time's a Wasting," a June 24, 1988 *USA Today* story, that's how much time we spend opening unsolicited mail!

2. **If you're overwhelmed with unwanted mail,** write to the Direct Marketing Association, P.O. Box 9008, Farmingdale, New York 11735 and ask that your name be removed from all catalog mailing lists. Mail-order firms check with DMA quarterly to purge their lists. Be sure to include any variations on name and address spellings. If there are catalogs you want, you'll need to contact them directly to receive their mailings, but specify that they cannot rent your name. In the meantime, resist the temptation to open everything that arrives in your mailbox. Mail that is obviously sales-mail goes directly into our recycling bins. Remember, no one is forcing you to open it and read it! By disciplining yourself, you will

soon be free of infoglut and can spend your time pursuing more joyful and creative endeavors.

3. **Put yourself on an imformation diet.** Decide how
much time you *really* need to spend daily gathering info
and stick to it. You may even want to try taking a day or
two off each week for a mind-cleansing info fast! This
form of mental flossing often leads to the discovery of
the most exciting kind of information—*your own ideas.*
When you make space in your life for some downtime
and avoid the constant bombardment of the media, you
create room for your own creative breakthroughs and
expression.

4. **Read what you really *have* to.** Skim, using highlighting
markers to help you retain information, especially if you
reread the highlighted portions after the first run-
through.

5. **Choose where you want to focus your attention and
stick to it.** As your interests change, update your personal table of contents.

Our friend Jim Sullivan learned how to cope with infoglut as a result of his experience as a landscaper. He
explains: "What the media gurus usually don't get
around to telling you is that to be of any use, information
has to be continually weeded, pruned, harvested, com-
posted, hybridized, reseeded, researched, shared, protected, fertilized, bought, sold, and given away.
Massaging a set of files is the information junkie's equiv-
alent of working in the garden. Clipping the newspaper
makes a file grow just like spreading manure makes the
garden grow. Pruning makes it strong and more productive. Weeding gets rid of the junk. Harvesting makes
room for the next crop."

Sullivan says that information junkies share another
problem with gardeners, the Information Zucchini Para-
dox—the tendency of an information system to produce
more information than you can possibly use. Here again
the information junkie has the same options as the gardener. "Compost it, feed it to the chickens, trash it, or

best of all, find someone who will let you give it away to them. Someone like you."

6. **Let go of feeling anxious about not knowing it all.** Remember that you live in the age of specialization and there's just too much information blasting away at you daily for anyone to be well informed on everything. By putting yourself on an information diet—and just consuming the most life-giving, nutritious, and vital information that feeds your mind and soul—you'll be taking a major step in nurturing your creativity.

Making small changes in how you deal with information will allow you to reap valuable rewards; large changes will change your life in exciting new ways. It takes practice to break old habits, especially ones that are as ingrained as how you access information.

But if you are to simplify your life to make room for creative expression, contemplation, play, relationships, and the resulting joy that feeds your soul, you must change the way you spend your time. The simpler you make your life, the more freedom you have. The more freedom you have, the more space you can create for living your life out loud. It's that simple.

FOUR

◆

CREATIVITY IN ACTION

We hope you have gained helpful ideas and insights in the preceding chapters and are excited about making your life as creative and meaningful as possible. This section is all about stretching yourself, taking action and doing it! All the tips, exercises, and inspiration in the world are no substitute for taking action. Execution is the key to unleashing your creative genius.

Too many lives are struck in neutral. People are afraid to make the changes and take the risks necessary to reclaim their creative birthrights. In interviews with people in their eighties and nineties, the most commonly voiced regret is "I should have taken more chances and had more experiences." These people advise: *"Take more risks. Make more mistakes. Be crazier. Take more trips. Eat more ice cream. Swim more rivers. Have more troubles and fewer imaginary ones. Stop living ahead of a day."*

This section shows you how and why it's so important for you to break through isolation into the richness and possibilities of present-day community. You will discover the importance of storytelling and ritual, two of the oldest and most important ways for knitting communities together through creative expression.

You will also encounter the joy of enriching your life through service. Volunteerism through service provides the perfect playground for creative experimentation as it enables you to take new risks with your talents in a safe, nonthreatening, and nurturing way. In the last chapter, "Staying on the Joy Track," you will learn about breaking down goals into bite-size pieces to make it easier for you to take action. You will design your own personal life plan to help you set goals, keep focused, and make even your wildest dreams come true.

Living your life out loud is about taking action with courage, commitment, and boldness. Only you can unleash your creativity. Only you can turn your wishes for a joyful life into reality.

14

Create Fuzzy Boundaries

We are all the same person trying to shake hands with ourselves.
—WAVY GRAVY

Being in community enables you to realize your highest creative potential and greatly enhances your ability to live your life out loud. Without the meaningful connection provided by community, your creativity quickly becomes stagnant and your joy level half full.

Embracing community can help you bring more joy into your life by expanding your personal and social network of people with similar interests and goals. It can enhance your creative powers by opening up gates of opportunity that make it safe for you to try new ways of expressing yourself. The possibilities for community are limited only by your imagination.

Psychotherapist Susan Campbell relates her experience of community:

> What community means to me is that everyone has a sense of the whole. Everyone cares about everybody else. Nobody's just out for themselves. There is a shared commitment to something.

I was on the University of Massachusetts full-time graduate faculty for ten years. We were a learning community. It was a very nourishing cycle. It brought out a lot of growth in both the students and the faculty. Having people who believe in you and people who have seen you grow helps you feel safe enough to take risks. It becomes an environment where everybody wants to be creative and wants to be themselves and be real with each other.

I have come to think of community as a kind of vitamin. The experience of connectedness with others is as necessary to a fully healthy life as the minimum daily amount of each of the essential vitamins is to a balanced diet.
—CLAUDE WHITMYER, *In the Company of Others: Making Community in the Modern World*

Community Is All Around You

Community fulfills a fundamental human need to belong— the primary sense of being connected and supported that provides camaraderie, intimacy, continuity, spiritual well-being, and feelings of psychological and physical security. Community is all around you and comes in all shapes and sizes. There are religious communities, intentional communities, small town communities, office communities, social and service clubs, virtual communities, and networks of all kinds.

While the possibility of community is everywhere, many people feel disconnected and isolated, yearning for community as if it were impossible to find in the information age. We often hear some version of the following: "I feel so isolated, and I really would like to know my neighbors. Instead, I just come home from work and veg out. I don't have any energy left over for the kids, let alone myself. How could I possibly help beautify the neighborhood or help feed the homeless? Important as these things are, if I did them my life would be a disaster."

This is an understandable attitude and one almost anyone living in our fast-paced world can relate to. However, once you join a community that fits with your life, you will not only be rewarded with more energy and vitality, you will end up with more quality time and the support and connection necessary for a more creative life. The tragedy of modern-day isolation is illustrated by this stranger than fiction story.

> **A**dele Gaboury, seventy-three, had great neighbors. They took care of her lawn, looked after her mail, and tended to broken pipes. They missed one item: she was dead, four years dead, in a pile of trash on her kitchen floor. The Worcester, Massachusetts woman was a noted recluse. Her brother made inquiries in 1989, but after locating a woman with the same last name in a nursing home, he assumed it was her.
>
> —From the *Press Democrat* top news stories of 1993

In our workshops and consulting work we often encounter people who long for more community in their lives but are feeling stuck about how to proceed. We have identified the following three requirements necessary in order to create community:

1. Know what you want
2. Make time
3. Reach out

Know What You Want

Many people live far away from their loved ones, come from dysfunctional families, or for many other reasons need to create new supportive situations for themselves. For instance, Salli's parents were middle-aged when she was born and have been dead for many years. She has one sister who lives thousands of miles away. Salli grew up in the Midwest in that nostalgic sort of neighborhood where neighbors kept an eye on each others' children and kids visited freely from house to house. Neighbors often sipped lemonade and enjoyed cookies together in the cool of a summer evening, shoveled snow together in the winter, left their homes unlocked, and were there for each other during good times and bad. Yet, Salli knew only people like her family, had no privacy, and was constantly reminded of the guiding principle of small town life in the 1950s: What will the neighbors think? Her experience of growing up is often idealized and romanticized as the way community "should be"; yet it was actually homogeneous and stifling. While secure and loving, it was not conducive to living her life out loud. She moved to California to create the community she longed for.

Because Salli had little family, she acutely felt the need to create one, especially since she had a young daughter. For many years she lived on a large ranch with several other families who were all committed to taking care of the land and raising their children together. Now in mid-life, Salli has created an extended family that includes others who share her passion for gardening.

> "Family members" share seeds and cuttings, catalogs and information, and we help in each other's gardens. Many of the roses and irises, pumpkins and tomatoes growing in my garden were given to me by members of my extended family, who often come by to pick a bouquet for a special occasion, help harvest the strawberries and raspberries, or weed the flower beds. Many of my friends are artists, and some of the flowers are used in their paintings and photographs. When my extended family comes for a meal, they often help harvest the lettuce, cucumbers, corn, and potatoes for dinner and pick lavish bouquets for the table. Friends from the city come to relax and be refreshed by nature. In addition to growing food and flowers, the garden is very nourishing to my soul. Always changing and full of magic and joy, the garden and my family are the main sources of my creative inspiration.

In spite of our differences we are the same. When we are stripped of our differences—our culture, our language, our race, and our color—we then come face to face with our oneness.

—THE DALAI LAMA

Padi is involved in a variety of communities that nurture her creativity: a service club, a professional association, a religious affiliation, a school community, and a new form of connection—a mentor group. Nearly five years ago, Padi and four other women who share similar professional interests came together to support each other emotionally and professionally.

> We get together once or twice monthly, and it's been extremely powerful for me: The time we share is used to talk about what's working in our lives or not, to get feedback on business issues, to brainstorm ideas for each other's projects, and to help each other celebrate our wins. We are all self-employed, most with home-based businesses, so it's easy to get isolated and myopic. I see my mentor group as a personal board of advisors who can help guide and support me in my creative risks and endeavors with love and objectivity.
>
> At the beginning of each year we have a ritual that has been wonderful for each of us. We go around in a circle, and one by one tell each other how we've seen each other grow over the past year. It's amazing how easily we discount or forget what we do! This loving acknowledgment and reminder from people who know you and care about you is incredible. Best of all, while everyone is talking, one of us takes notes about what everyone says, and gives it to "the honoree of the moment" before moving onto the next group member. I keep this list of my accomplishments on my desk, and it's become an important reference point, especially during those times I feel stuck. Talk about building self-esteem through community! This mentor group has elevated mine. And that's encouraged me to take more creative risks in my work.

━━━━━━━━━━━━━━━━ **EXERCISE** ━━━━━━━━━━━━━━━━

What communities do you belong to? Include service clubs, computer networks, civic organizations, school, spiritual, work, professional organizations, etc.

Do these communities give you a satisfying feeling of connection and possibilities, or are they something you pursue from habit? Is it time to increase or decrease your involvement or find a new community to join? Rate them on a scale of 1 to 10, with 1 being top priority and 10 being lowest.

━━━━━━━━━━━━━━━━ **EXERCISE** ━━━━━━━━━━━━━━━━

Think of the most satisfying communities you have ever been part of. Whether it was helping to operate a co-op nursery school for your children, volunteering once a week at a soup kitchen, or living in a dorm your freshman year at college, this exercise will remind you of community situations that have nourished you in the past.

Imagine the perfect community situation for yourself at this time using what you learned above.

When one of our single workshop participants did this exercise, she realized how much she missed the Sunday dinners of her youth, complete with mashed potatoes and gravy and a big slice of pie plus lots of caring friendly faces around the dining room table. Karen shared the desire to recreate this ritual with some of her friends, and to her delight several responded that they loved the idea. Once she identified the community she wanted, Karen was able to help create what she calls a "voluntary family" that happily share dinner every Sunday evening.

Making Time

The second key to creating community is making time. Our lives have become too much regimented by lines in appointment books and "tight" schedules. Rushing around without making time for other people makes for an empty life. Creativity and joy need the fuel that a community of friends and peers provides. We need to take the time just to *be* together sharing the important moments of our lives along with the more subtle experiences of day-to-day life.

We don't drop in on each other much anymore. There are few casual impromptu social moments. Spontaneity is nearly extinct. The price we have paid for this privacy and compartmentalization is a loss of intimacy and joy. We cannot really know each other if we don't share a range of experience, and we cannot share a range of experience if we are isolated and all our social interaction is controlled.

> For the preservation and transmission of the fundamentals of civilization, vigorous, wholesome community life is imperative. Unless many people live and work in the intimate relationships of community life, there can never emerge a truly unified nation, or a community of mankind.
>
> If I do not love my neighbor whom I know, how can I love the human race? . . . If I have not learned to work with a few people, how can I be effective with many?
> —ARTHUR E. MORGAN

Faith Morgan, the granddaughter of Arthur E. Morgan, grew up in a community in Yellow Springs, Ohio, founded by her parents. This intentional community was comprised of Quaker families who chose to live and work cooperatively, to create a life that reflected their shared values. An artist and CEO of a computer software company, Faith's childhood memories are rich with the natural sharing that comes from living in close proximity with others. When asked what keeps people from realizing the support and connection that comes from community, Faith replied, "The first thing to look at is how people spend their time. If you're overly busy, you often don't feel like being with your friends. Instead you'll watch TV when you come home after work.

> I have made community a priority all of my life, arranged my work so that I could always take time off and go to Yellow Springs and visit with my other friends around the

country and to help my neighbors when they needed me. Recently, however, I have been in this situation where the business is taking all of my brain power and time. When I have a little bit of time, I just flake out. . . . I realize how damaging this is to what is really meaningful in my life.

I have rearranged my work so that I can take an art class. So instead of working eighty hours a week in the corporate scene and that's all there is in my life, I am taking all day Fridays to paint and be with my friends. These are the things that feed other parts of me. Now, for the first time in a while, I dream about painting instead of spread sheets and packages getting mailed out and software, and that's a wonderful change for me. I now feel a balance in my life, and I'm enjoying everything so much more. I have made time in my life for community and my art.

Donna Freeman, activist and businesswoman, has a large family but still manages to make community a priority. She smiled when she told us of an entire weekend party she hosted last June in her garden:

There were about sixty of us. All of the people we invited had been special in our lives. We are all hitting our mid-fifties. Some people hadn't seen each other in twenty-five years. We barbequed all the seafoods we could get. Our kids had reserved that weekend to serve and prepare the food, so we didn't have to leave our guests. After dinner on Saturday night someone got out the guitar, and we told stories from forty years ago. We just had the best time.

At brunch the next day we had a memorial service for two sets of friends who had recently lost sons in their twenties. Their parents planted rhododendrons in their memory. Six weeks later, the man who was the master of ceremonies at the service died. While I was in Washington last week, I lost another old friend who had been at the party, and I just found out that another friend is dying of a brain tumor. Three people from that weekend. That's a lot of people out of such a small gathering. Thank God we had that get-together.

Donna's story is a reminder to treasure those important people in our lives by making them a priority. "I keep in touch through the telephone," Donna told us. "I'm probably the one that keeps us all together. My claim to fame is that I do put out that effort to gather everybody in. I have wonderful friends. I am really blessed. The world would be different if people paid more attention to their friends. People just get too busy." It's become all too commonplace to put friends and family on hold, assuming they will understand, that they will always be there. You can't hug a job. No amount of riches can take the place of a friend. It's not difficult to make time for community—it just needs to go into your 10% category. The rewards are stronger relationships and a sense of well-being, both of which enhance your ability to be creative and more joyful.

Reaching Out

If you were going to die soon and had only one phone call you could make, who would you call and what would you say? And why are you waiting?

STEPHEN LEVINE

The old paradigm of the rugged individualist makes it difficult to create community; it masks our vulnerability, our need for one another—causing us to isolate ourselves, pretending we don't need anyone else. Fortunately, in spite of our tenacious individualism, in spite of our reluctance to reach out, the possibility for community is all around us—we just need to take the risk. It doesn't have to be a big risk. Try reaching out to those who are already a part of your life. When writing or speaking about community, Arthur E. Morgan emphasized that the beginning point of community is person-to-person relationship and that we must first learn to live in harmony with the people closest to us.

In the early 1970s many young people were creating communities in which to live their values, raise their children together, and act as stewards of the land. Salli was part of such a community and fondly remembers her friendship with neighbor Pete Albini, an Italian farmer who lived his lived his entire life in rural northern California.

> When we "back-to-the-landers" moved into this tiny community, the neighbors were very suspicious of us newcomers with our long hair and bizarre clothing and our thinking we could learn to farm from a book. They gave us a wide berth. Not Pete. He tried his best to help us with both the practical and spiritual aspects of country living. It couldn't have been easy. We were so naive, so full of our own romantic notions. But Pete patiently showed us how to run a tractor, raise a lamb abandoned by its mom, cut the eyes of a potato just so for planting, how to mow the hay, make our own cheese, and in general see what was going on around us.
>
> Pete had his own family to raise and worked the land from sunrise to dusk, but he was always willing to lend a hand when anybody needed him. By his example he taught us what it meant to live together in community. The best advice he ever gave to me was: "In any trade always give more than you get." I knew this advice went beyond just practical matters. To me it meant to bend a little further and risk a little more and to always be willing to reach out to others.

EXERCISE

You don't need a master's degree in community to reach out to others. Who do you know right now who could use a caring phone call, a visit, an offer of help? Take a moment and think of all the people you have been meaning to call—choose one and say hello. Invite someone you have been missing over for brunch and treat him like the extra special person he is—your friend. Make a card and send it to someone you haven't seen in a long time; tell her how important she is in your life. If someone you know just graduated or got a promotion or scored a life win, drop him or her a note saying how proud you are.

Once you know the kind of community experience that is missing or needs enriching in your life, it's up to you to reach out to others and make it happen. You can't just sit there and hope people will seek you out. Donna Freeman realized this when she moved to a small community far from her home. She remembers:

> I had a newborn son who was literally sixteen hours old when I was dropped off in a new community. I knew two people. I had no phone. Everything was still in boxes. I had a baby twenty-one months old and another almost four years old. I cried for an entire year the first year I was here because my husband was a fisherman and gone all the time. Once I stopped feeling sorry for myself and decided to meet people, I haven't had a boring day since.

For Ruth Stotter, storytelling is an important way to reach out to create community. She recalls the sense of connectedness that resulted when she told stories in a local bookstore:

> In the bookstore people would come who didn't know each other, because it was a safe place for singles. And then two weeks later you might recognize someone and go sit at their table because you saw them there before. You bonded because you had been on the same adventure, the same emotional experience. So you felt like you were old friends even though you hadn't exchanged a word before. There's something important that happens when you bring people together so we're not all these lonely little vessels. We connect and come together as a group. My goal in life has always been to take separate individuals and turn them into a group.

Feeling Good by Doing Good

Love is something if you give it away, you end up getting more.
—MALVINA REYNOLDS

One of the most rewarding ways of reaching out into your community and making heartfelt connections is through service. Volunteering is a creative growth experience. Service provides mutual nourishment and builds community in deep ways by dissolving artificial barriers between people. There are many reasons people volunteer, but top of the list is wanting to make a difference by doing something useful. Although volunteering usually begins with wanting to contribute to the community, the more service work you do, the more you realize the personal benefits. You not only learn new skills, but you learn more about yourself and the world around you.

A new perspective on life, new skills, new friends, new connections, and increased self-esteem and creativity are just some of the benefits that come from serving others. By exercising compassion you not only open yourself to new possibilities, your ability to experience joy deepens. One of the most meaningful human connections you can make is through service.

Creative Cross-Training

Service is an opportunity to grow new dendrites—which make creative connections in the brain—through cross-training. According to brain researcher Dr. Marian Cleeves Diamond, "Positive interaction with people is terribly important. Helping others helps us grow, and we'll grow better creatively and intellectually."

If you want to try out new skills, volunteering may present an opportunity to do so in a low-risk, safe, and pressure-free environment. When you let your creativity out into your community and do it for free, it takes away some of the fear of judgment by others, because the recipients' expectations are different.

Sara Winge of the Santa Rosa, California, Volunteer Center agrees:

> Volunteering allows you to stretch and try new things. To express different parts of yourself that you might not usually be able to do. It can be as simple as doing the decorations for an event or preparing a gourmet meal to raise money for your children's school. Volunteering can also provide a way to build new skills. For example, in this ever-shifting job situation, if you wanted to work in human resources, you might volunteer to be on a human resources commission to become familiar with what that would require. It would help you understand what the work really entails, develop the necessary skills, and let you see if this is the way you want to spend your time.

As a professional speaker, Padi never experiments with new material on clients—but will take the risk of a joke bombing or a story not being quite perfected during an occasional free presentation for a service organization or volunteer professional group. The risk is lower, and she can experiment more comfortably. Volunteerism is a way to try new things or take creative risks in safe ways, while doing something to enhance another's life.

Salli's sister, Jean Ruwe, always wanted to play an instrument and finally took the leap at age sixty through the safe channel of service. Jean remembers:

> As a child I was encouraged only for my artistic talents, and while I enjoy my art, when I reached sixty I decided that if I were going to try my musical wings I had better start! I joined a dulcimer group, and we perform all over the area. These performances include playing for patients in a locked mental ward, for recovering stroke patients, preschool children, schools, libraries, historic centers, churches, senior centers, and others. Our current program is teaching G.E.D. students about the dulcimer and its music. These are Appalachian persons with little or no self-esteem. Our goal is to install pride in their Appalachian

culture by teaching them the history of their music and helping them to learn to play the dulcimer. We even have a Christmas tape on the market. Last year we performed in over seventy-five programs.

EXERCISE

Grow new dendrites. What skills would you like to improve or develop in a new low-risk context? Call your local volunteer center and ask which agencies could use the talents you want to practice. Set a date to begin. Go for it!

When Salli's mother was dying, her family was helped tremendously by Hospice. Her sister, Jean, was so impressed with the organization that she helped found the music program at the Hospice of Cincinnati, Ohio.

Sometimes I bring my dulcimer and play for ambulatory patients and their families. The dulcimer is one of the instruments most highly recommended for music therapy. Many of the patients are comatose or in the dying process so we play soft music or relaxation tapes in the rooms as it is said that the hearing is acute at these times. Music seems to calm the restless and also helps the families.

I come home from hospice feeling very rewarded by the patients themselves. The volunteers pray, feed the patients, care for them, and allay their fears. The patients' words of thanks or a smile or seeing them relax and lose some of their fears is ample payment for our time.

Through serving others, Jean has found a way to unleash her long-buried musical creativity, as well as make positive contribution in the lives of so many. The joy she gives others only increases her own.

Artist Miller Phoenix teaches art to dying patients because:

I want to encourage them to take color and movement and their own symbols and transcend to the next reality. I also gain insight that I would not have gotten all by myself.

When I give of myself I observe the reaction, and I get back information that I never would have had through teaching a formal class or any other experience. I take more risks. I don't have that agenda or structure that I have to follow in a class and I don't have any rules because I'm on my own. Service feeds my personal creativity because the more I can feel I'm doing for other people, the more energy comes back to me. The more energy comes through me as a painter and the more creative I become.

Service is the great illuminator; the more we serve, the wiser we become. . . . Only those who serve are those who truly live.
—LIM CHIN HIN, *Rotarian*

What is it about serving others that gives so much to the giver? Why do volunteers feel their experiences helping others have made a significant contribution to their own happiness? New scientific research has proven what must of us know intuitively: helping others produces healing, happy biochemical changes for the doer. Helping doesn't just feel good, it *is* good for you. As Allan Luks reported in *The Healing Power of Doing Good,* in a national survey 95% of volunteers said that helping others on a regular basis gave them an immediate feel-good sensation, a "helper's high," which is a powerful rush resulting in an increased sense of euphoria and energy. Volunteers also noted improvements in their own health and experienced increased feelings of self-worth.

As the former director of a volunteer services network, Jude Winerip has had a lot of experience with helper's high. She explains:

Helper's high is that feeling of satisfaction you get when you know you've been effective. It's not about taking over somebody's life. Its not about doing something for somebody that they're capable of doing. It's being able to be of assistance to somebody and walk with them through it rather than take control of a situation that they could otherwise be in control of themselves.

Probably my most memorable helper's high experience—one that was wonderful and painful at the same time—was with a terminally ill man who contacted our office one day. He was in tears and pretty much falling apart. He was awakened in the middle of the night to his chickens squawking their heads off and realized that a raccoon had gotten into his chicken coop. By morning most of the chickens were either dead or dying. He didn't have the faintest idea what to do. He kept saying, "I can't cope with this. I don't know what to do."

I went with him to his house, and when I got there he gave me an old pair of pants and an old shirt and a pair of his shoes, and I went up and cleaned out that chicken coop. I took the chickens that were almost dead and put them in a crate because I knew they were going to die pretty soon anyway, and I took the ones that were totally dead and buried them. Then I cleaned everything up. It was one of those times when you know what you need to do and you do it and you feel incredibly wonderful while you're doing it, but it was . . . what do they call the Peace Corps? "One of the hardest jobs you'll ever love." It was kind of like that.

Service to others is the rent you pay for living on this planet.
—MARIAN WRIGHT EDELMAN

Reuben Weinzveg is a volunteer trustee of a land trust that provides permanent protection of land and its resources. Since their inception, land trusts have preserved thousands of acres of agricultural and open space land. Reuben feels enriched by his work with the land trust because it provides him with a connection to something in the community that he cherishes. One of the reasons Reuben loves the work he has done with the Sonoma Land Trust is that he knows that when he has helped to protect open space or habitat on a particular property, that land is protected forever. It is the sense of "forever" that gives him particular pleasure in his volunteer work. Instead of being negative and frustrated about all the land that is being lost to development, Reuben can "do something that's very important to me, be effective, and know it's forever."

Reuben is also a gardener and speaks of the joy of growing something in the garden as a metaphor for the high obtained from community service. "You get the experience of working in the garden as well as the by-products of good-tasting, wholesome food, beautiful flowers, creating an aesthetic statement, and the joy of sharing it all with those you love," he explains. "Look at what you get to participate in. The seed that you plant contains the miracle, but you get to be there."

Finding Your Right Service

What makes you mad? What makes your blood boil? What tugs at your heart strings? The state of the environment? Abused children? The elderly infirm isolated in nursing homes? The illiteracy rate? Teenage suicide? The homeless?

Where do you want to stretch yourself creatively? What new skills would you like to learn? By matching your creative talents with a cause you believe in, you can discover service that will bring more joy and love into your life. Before you rush out to volunteer, ask yourself what you want out of the experience. There are so many options: blood donor, crisis phone counselor, foster grandparent, peer counselor, braille transcriber, companion to shut-in, suicide hot-line counselor, and unlimited spontaneous volunteerism. Even if you only have an hour a week, or an hour a month, you can make a difference by including service in your 10%.

There are hundreds of volunteer centers that can match up your interests and talents with worthy organizations who need people just like you. If your town is too small, contact a nearby metropolitan area for a list of agencies. The reference desk at your local library can help you find agencies such as Retired Senior Volunteer Programs (RSVP), Big Brothers and Big Sisters in your area.

Sara Winge notes:

Volunteering is a tool that builds relationships in a lovely way. It makes the web of life richer. People from many different places come together as peers, possibilities are opened up, and connections are made. You are given a broad picture of life when you volunteer.

Every year we have our volunteer appreciation luncheon where each group picks their volunteer of the year. I am always incredibly touched and inspired with the litany of wonderful people doing incredible things. Invariably the volunteers say "I get more out of this than the people I'm serving."

Reuben Weinzveg agrees: "If you change just one soul or give someone a boost that changes their life, you have the satisfaction of having done something for the world."

We make a living by what we get. We make a life by what we give.
—WINSTON CHURCHILL

Jude Winerip thinks what motivates people to volunteer is different depending on whom they are deciding to volunteer with or what the work is.

Definitely I think it's always self-motivated. Whether it's political or spiritual or to physically challenge yourself in some way. Whether it's about planting trees or cleaning up the beach or going to visit seniors in a convalescent home or helping rid your neighborhood of crime, I feel it's all the same. I think that people want to reach out, they want to help someone else regardless of how little or how much they have themselves. People want to connect with somebody else, and they want to feel like they are doing their part.

EXERCISE

Sometimes it's just nice to help someone anonymously. Send an inspirational poem or quote, flowers, or even a cashier's check to someone you know who needs a boost but is too proud or shy to ask. Imagine the joy the recipient will receive by your loving and creative gesture.

Kate Bishop recently began volunteering. "I just started becoming aware that I've been well paid for my work, and I have a lot to share. I really want to get something other than money for my work. I want to feel like I'm doing somebody some good."

The thing that has just naturally cropped up in my life is the AIDS issue and the Names Project Quilt. My friend Patrick works for the post office and wanted to do a quilt panel for postal employees who have been affected by AIDS and have it come out with the dedication of the new AIDS awareness stamp. He asked me to work with him on it. It was wonderful doing it. We had to cut out these little letters and affix them onto the quilt panel that said "AIDS Awareness." I went through a lot of different technical means of doing it before I hit on the right one, and in the process I accidentally transferred the words "AIDS Awareness" onto my worktable and other surfaces in my studio. As I worked on it the words kind of sunk in, and I found that in the process of doing this, all the emotions I had put off experiencing came up for me. I developed AIDS awareness, that is what happened. Since then I've worked on two other quilt panels. It seems like a good service project for me. I can be available to the families of people who have been lost to AIDS, or just be available as a technical advisor on how to do a quilt panel. I feel I'm putting something back into the pool. It's wonderful.

People find working with people with AIDS, or anyone who is terminally ill, emotionally and spiritually rewarding. Working with somebody who is dying generally exposes you to the ultimate truth in their life, because there's really nothing for them to hide anymore. So you are with somebody in an incredibly vulnerable and honest place of truth. And the amount of opening of heart that can happen is really extraordinary.

Kate Harrison has another perspective:

What really struck me when my dad was dying was that many of our parents have died, are dying, or are going to die. And there will be more and more of the need for us to sit by bedsides with dying people, and for that to be done for us, too. That wasn't part of our rosy 1960s view of how life was supposed to be. But it's as real as it gets. And it's beautiful as long as you're not doing it with fear and denial.

Sitting through a friend's birth or being in labor yourself . . . and then sitting with death . . . they're not that different.

Giving and Receiving

Learning to receive is just as valuable as learning to give. At some point in our lives, each of us will need help and support. Serving others also prepares us for receiving in the future.

"I look at giving for the long term," Sara Winge remarks. "Everyone uses services in their life. It's so much a part of the fabric of life. You might give today, but tomorrow you or your mother or sister or someone else close to you will be receiving."

Giving seems to come easier than receiving. Most of us need practice in asking for help and feeling comfortable being on the receiving end. Yet, when we give others the opportunity to help us, when we become more vulnerable, and open to receiving, we learn to be more sensitive to others—and therefore even more willing to be there for them. In a way it's selfish *not* to receive, because we are depriving others of helper's high and learning new skills and all the other benefits of volunteering. So if someone offers to help, by all means let them have the pleasure of doing so!

Universal truth: What goes around comes around.

EXERCISE

It should be as comfortable to give as to receive. How have you been helped recently? What were the circumstances? How did it feel to be on the receiving end? Did you help someone recently? What were the circumstances? How did it feel to be on the giving end?

Salli's friend Mary is a talented landscape designer who enjoys helping people in their gardens. She not only designed a special rock wall garden area for Salli, but took the time to find the healthiest plants and put them in herself. Every few weeks Mary comes over and weeds the new garden addition. Initially, Salli felt uneasy and concerned about how she could possibly repay her friend. Because she knows how good it feels to help others, however, Salli decided instead to relax and enjoy this wonderful gift, knowing that her friend loves her and is herself enriched by the experience.

Be kind, for everyone you meet is fighting a hard battle.

—PLATO

EXERCISE

Just say yes. Do you let others give to you? Notice how you react when someone gives you a compliment or offers to help you. Next time someone reaches out to you by offering help or a compliment, accept their gift graciously, knowing that it makes them happy, too. A simple "Thank you" or "Yes! I'd love your help" is a gift in return.

Faith Morgan grew up in a community where giving and receiving were a way of life. "In our community there were lots of people with what I call 'fuzzy boundaries,' who would just naturally help each other," Faith recalls.

For instance, my dad died recently. I did some arranging, but basically people came out of the woodwork and helped organize everything that needed to be done. Nobody had to ask, it just sort of happened. They felt like part of a family. They cared and just came out and helped. That's community.

Because I grew up where people did share and take care of and help out, I just assumed that was the way life was. I think if you didn't have that experience you would feel a lot of emptiness. And I think much of our culture does feel an emptiness—lots of boundaries to naturalness. When people grow up and see themselves as really isolated, it's hard for giving and receiving to come naturally. You learn to keep score when someone does something for you and you return every favor. You resist letting others help you because even though you need the help, you will then feel beholden. It feels so good once you realize there is a bounty and that giving and receiving is part of the universe, part of the way things function.

This old Jewish story tells the value of service in simple, metaphoric terms.

HEAVEN AND HELL

A rabbi died and went to be with God. God decided to give him a tour of his domain. First the Good Lord showed him to hell. They entered a large room where a group of people sat around a huge aromatic pot of stew. Everyone was famished and desperate. Each held a spoon that reached the pot, but each spoon had a handle so long that it could not be used to reach the person's mouth. The cries of suffering were awful!

The Lord then took him to heaven. They entered another room, identical to the first: the same pot of fragrant stew, a group of people, the same long spoons. But there everyone was happy and nourished.

"I don't understand," said the rabbi. "Why are they happy here when they were miserable in the other room and everything was just the same?" The Lord smiled. "Ah, don't you see?" He said, "Here they have learned to feed each other."

It is one of the most beautiful compensations in life that no man can truly help another without helping himself.

—RALPH WALDO EMERSON

Serving others helps strengthen your creativity by providing low-risk avenues of self-expression while making a difference in the lives of others. The joy of giving, the joy of creating, and the joy of helping come from service.

The most essential thing in life is to establish an unafraid, heartfelt connection with others.

—SOGYAL RIMPOCHE, *Tibetan Book of Living and Dying*

Community keeps us vital and healthy. When we create a balance between satisfying our needs as individuals and the needs of our community, we feel complete. Our natural communities have been washed over by modern society. During the time that we were immersed in community and slowly lost it, the world changed around us, and we must now create what used to come naturally.

In order to survive as a nation we *must* learn to cooperate with and to trust one another. In a speech at the University of Texas in April of 1993, Hillary Rodham Clinton called on all Americans "to be willing to remold society by redefining what it means to be a human being." The First Lady, speaking of a national "sleeping sickness of the soul" said, "We lack some core-level meaning in our individual lives, and meaning collectively—that sense that our lives are part of some greater effort, that we are connected to one another."

The individual is what he is and has the significance that he has not so much in virtue of this individuality, but rather as a member of a great human community, which directs his material and spiritual existence from the cradle to the grave.

—ALBERT EINSTEIN

We feel very passionate about the need to create the New American Community. This will require a shift in our national mindset, however, since independence and individual freedom is the hallmark of our nation. Clearly this rugged individualism stuff isn't working. We are so starved for community, we are literally dying for it. Isolated and disconnected people who no longer feel they have a stake in the world are not only a threat to themselves and society—their unique contribution will be tragically lost forever.

At this point in history the creative contribution of everyone is greatly needed. As social networks crumble around us it is paramount that we create nurturing, sustainable communities. While it's important to celebrate and appreciate the importance of each individual, it's equally important that we recognize and value the importance of community. We need each other!

Ron Jones, author, playwright, storyteller, and physical education director at the acclaimed San Francisco Recreation Center for the Handicapped, sent the following story to his friends at Christmas:

THE MOONBEAM CHRISTMAS: A TRUE STORY

San Francisco's most unusual Christmas tree isn't in Union Square or the window of some California Street Victorian. In fact, it might not even be a tree.

For the past seven years, the Moonbeams, a group of mentally disabled adults at the Recreation Center for the Handicapped, have made ornaments and then set out to find and decorate a special tree. This year's annual pilgrimage discovered a scraggly bush. It was perfect. Not tall enough to be a tree. Or beautiful enough to be considered a flower. But it was along a city park path. The same path they walked on every Tuesday. And it was alone. Undistinguished. Waiting to be chosen. To be momentarily adored as the source of joy for all those that pass by. You see, that was the Moonbeams' gift to San Francisco.

Each year, the Moonbeams decorate their tree and silently enjoy the smiles of joggers slowing before the shimmer of tinsel. They watch as dogs, accustomed to one-leg stands, push their wet noses against the reflecting tin plates. And old-timers give a knowing nod to this vision of something done for the pleasure of doing it. This is their gift. The most unusual Christmas tree. This moment of surprise and wonder in a world of predictability and caution.

This year, something strange happened. When the Moonbeams returned to their tree, they found a surprise. Dangling from the branches of their tree and intermixed with their handmade decorations, they saw store-bought ornaments. And ribbons tied in a bow. Someone had placed a plastic strawberry basket on one of the branches. And there was an aluminum pull tab shining like a miniature halo. And cards—all manner of cards—declared a special season's greeting. An insurance salesman's card said simply, "Yea, Yea." Other cards had traditional scenes and messages. "Merry Christmas, from the Carolyns." One message was particularly appreciated. It read. "Thank you, whoever you are—this is the only gift I got. God bless you. God bless us all."

And it is still true, no matter how old you are, when you go out into the world, it is better to hold hands and stick together.

—ROBERT FULGHUM, *All I Ever Really Needed to Know I Learned in Kindergarten*

15

Rediscover the Joy of Ritual and Storytelling

Western man has purchased prosperity at the cost of a staggering impoverishment of the vital elements of life. These elements are festivity—the capacity for genuine revelry and joyous celebration—and fantasy—the faculty for envisioning radically alternative life situations.

—HARVEY COX

Two of the oldest and most important ways for knitting communities together and passing on our deepest values are ritual and storytelling. We aren't sure why people stopped valuing their authentic stories and began to devalue ritual. All we know is that we want them back in our lives!

Rejoice in Ritual

Ritual provides us with rich opportunities to coalesce as a community and to rejoice in life's rhythms. It compounds our joy as we mark significant passages, and it diminishes our sorrow during times of pain. Ritual is the affirmation of community and one of the most important vehicles for connecting us to one another and the earth. Ritual also provides us with a rich vehicle for expressing our creativity. Designing meaningful rituals can be highly creative, as it can include many art forms: music, dance, poetry, chanting or singing, decorating, arts and crafts, mask making, ceremonial food preparation, and more.

Rituals and celebrations remind us of the magic and mystery of life. They form the golden links in our connections with one another. The more connections, the more we fertilize the soil for our creativity to grow. Yet, in our sped-up world we too often fail to mark important occasions, passages, and transitions. By failing to give ourselves the time for celebration, in effect we give no attention or value to what is most significant in our lives.

The cycles of life and death have been whisked away from us. We have become increasingly removed from the rhythm of life as our species knew it until about a hundred years ago. We birth in sterile hospitals; our babies are often put behind glass to be admired. We die in hospitals cared for by strangers; our remains are handled by anonymous rubber-gloved death technicians who never knew us. Even our food is irradiated, the nutrients being zapped in favor of longer shelf life at the supermarket. It's as if everything that resonates with the essence of life has become whitewashed or sterilized in the name of efficiency and progress.

This cultural sanitization is not healthy; emotionally, spiritually, or physically. We believe that the epidemic proportions of depression in this country stem in large part from cultural sanitization, the isolation from ourselves, our communities, the environment. The loss of innocence, wonder, and reverence for the mystery of life has created disenfranchisement for millions of people.

When we celebrate the seasons and how they affect the earth and our own survival, we are reenacting a sacred and ancient ritual. We have become aloof from the environment, and rituals help to remind us how powerful and nurturing this necessary connection is. We are not designed to live in the society we have created, cut off from plants and animals and the earth itself. We know this in our bones, and ritual provides an important vehicle to reconnect with the land and one another.

In our melting pot nation, ancestral traditions and rituals are forgotten, diluted, or no longer seem relevant. With families scattered geographically, there is often little reinforcement and few role models to carry on ethnic, religious, and oral traditions. Many of our rituals have lost their sparkle, have become hollow and without substance.

Yet, according to ceramicist, Leslie Gattman, ritual doesn't have to be rigid or hollow. "There can be a lot of creativity to ritual. Most religions have a long, historic root system based on thousands of years of history, so you can choose to focus on one aspect or another. Today, there's a whole group of people recreating ritual to fit into their lifestyles."

Leslie and her husband, Eugene Frank, have combined their love of ritual and art into a unique business called Ceramic Judaica. From their California wine country home and studio, they create Jewish ritual art; beautifully hand-crafted porcelain holiday platters, candlesticks, and other items for ceremonial use.

"There are universal anxieties—aloneness, meaningfulness, need for love," explains Eugene, formerly a psychotherapist before joining Leslie in the business thirteen years ago. "Those are the things most people struggle with on and off throughout their lives. People are uncomfortable with the scatteredness of life. There are so many choices; people end up turning toward something that can give them structure to deal with the strong emotions of life."

Adding one's own creative touches to that structure can make ritual resonate with greater meaning. At the Gattman-Frank household, the Jewish ritual of lighting candles on Friday nights to welcome the Sabbath has been given a new twist. "After the blessing of the wine, we say what the best part of the week was for each of us," says Leslie. "This is especially nice because it makes us all think about what we did; we get to reflect together. It's very nice for the kids. It's one way we're at peace together at the end of the week."

Ritual can be as creatively elaborate or simple as you care to make it. Some rituals occur once in a lifetime, such as a rite of passage, or they can be daily occurrences such as morning meditation or giving thanks before meals. Ritual can be something you do over and over without energy, almost like a duty, but it can be so much more than that. When we pay attention to the details and invest parts of ourselves in a ritual, it comes alive for us. When you fully participate and focus on the moment, the creative possibilities open up. An ordinary potluck dinner and meeting becomes revitalized and takes on creative dimensions when a theme is chosen, for example. Suddenly what might have been a ho-hum obligation is turned into something exciting and fun. It's the personal investment of energy that makes the difference. Watching the Chinese New Year Parade is lots of fun, for instance, but embroidering a special garment, learning a dance, decorating a float for the parade, and enjoying specially prepared food afterward is where the creativity and joyfulness come from. Many rituals that have become habits can, by a slight creative shift, significantly enrich our lives.

There is a quiet groundswell of people who are creating their own celebrations, inventing and adapting rituals that have real meaning for their lives. To help inspire you to create your own rituals and meaningful traditions, here is a sampling of our favorites from people interviewed for this book.

A Rite of Passage

"A rite of passage need not be complicated or difficult to do. Its value is created simply in doing it. Taking the time is the important thing," reflects Robert Brent after orchestrating the celebration of his son's transition from boyhood to manhood. After his son Bailey attended a Bar Mitzvah for his friend, he told his dad that he thought it was wonderful that "all those people stopped whatever they were doing to pay attention to a kid."

Robert set about to plan an appropriate celebration. But because his son is a mixture of nationalities and religious backgrounds, there were no clear guidelines. "I wanted our ceremony to be simple to plan and based in the traditions and culture of our ancestors. I wanted a family affair . . . based on a day with just the men in the family and close male friends who had relationships both with me and with Bailey."

On a Saturday in October, all the men in Bailey's family and one adult friend met at the Brent home. As Robert had written to each participant before the event: "We are gathering to give Bailey our attention for a day, to notice his growth, to let him know about the rights, privileges, and obligations of a man in the family and in society, without an expectation of immediate change in him. We can show him how we value him and look forward to his process of growing up."

The day began with a tree-planting ceremony, to symbolize how families continue through time. Robert selected a tree that will be ideal for climbing and building a tree house in after fifteen years, when Bailey may have his own children to enjoy it. After planting, a time capsule was buried at the base of the tree, and each guest brought a small token to put inside the capsule—something that would be fun to unearth decades from now.

After lunch, the group headed for the old family ranch, a 120-acre spread that was settled by Bailey's great-great-grandfather in 1868. Stories of barn dances, raising pigs, and Bailey's great-great-grandfathers, who were both tanners and knew each other well, filled the afternoon and gave Bailey a sense of history of the generations of men who lived before him.

After dinner, a ritual of gift giving began. Robert began with a gift he had received from his maternal grandfather. He told a story about him and his life as a businessman. Robert talked about his sacrifices for his children, his disappointments, and his admonishments about the duties of a man in the family. The gift was a sterling silver mechanical pencil with Robert's name engraved on it, which seemed perfect for Bailey, since art is his primary interest. Other gifts followed, each given with much thought and special significance. As each gift was given, the men shared stories from their hearts.

For the closing ritual, father asked son to rise and stand in the middle of the circle of men. Each man then rose and stood close around him. Each putting a hand on his shoulder, Robert said to his son, "Bailey, we all welcome you and accept you into the society of men and as a man in the family."

A Time to Die

Less than one hundred years ago there were no funeral homes. The deceased were kept at home until they were buried. Families cleaned, dressed, and buried their own dead.

When Kate Luna's seventy-year-old uncle died, she and her family decided that *they* should prepare his body for burial. "The decision was made that there would be no embalming. Uncle Ace would be dressed by his son and a friend. Since Ace was a surfer, he would wear his white sweatshirt and khakis. It was a great struggle with the funeral directors, who wanted to "spare the family the pain" and handle the body themselves. My cousin threatened to walk out, taking the clothes and the body with him," Kate recalls.

Kate finds the idea of "sparing the family pain" ironic; "I think of my aunt, who has miscarried, buried a mother, a father, a son, who has known this man as lover for over fifty years. What is there left to be protected from?"

She recalls the day of funeral preparation:

Everyone was ready to risk the reality because something important had bound us together. This is family. We risk our private terror, the unknown, the vulnerability of making sounds of grief we've never made aloud before in the company of each other. We have to hold each other, as knees give way to grief and howling sadness. Each in our own time reaches out and touches the body, so familiar but now so cold.

We place our hands on his cold, cold skin and with our warmth, warm him so he can be dressed. Boy cousins and dearest male friends stay to unwrap the sheets and massage his limbs to make it possible to dress him for our last time together.

They lined his coffin with his Balinese sarong and placed a basket of fruit at his feet. "He was forever peeling and slicing and taking bites out of fruit and life." Kate remembers. Each family member then placed a reminder gift in the coffin: his favorite book and hat, surf booties, poems by his grandson, the bill for the high-priced airline tickets purchased for family who flew in for the funeral on short notice.

What often turns out to be a hollow, morbid experience became a celebration of life. By taking control of Ace's funeral and dealing with the reality of his corpse, Kate's family experienced an extremely intimate connection with loved ones, sharing their sorrow and pain, and reflecting upon the joy they had known with Ace.

Mary Reid participated in a spontaneous ritual that helped her and her terminally ill mother say good-bye. Mary's mother had been ill for a long time and was dying at home. One day while Mary was visiting her mother, the old woman began to talk about her past in a way she had never done before. While deep into her reminiscing, she asked her daughter to look in the back of her closet. Mary was surprised to find a collection of very old clothing in mint condition.

The dresses were lovingly hung in plastic garment bags with faded tissue between them. Her mother had saved every special-occasion dress she had worn as an adult! Each one still smelled sweet with the perfume that was popular that year.

"Would you please put on my wedding dress, dear?" the older woman asked. "You look so much like I used to look." As Mary modeled for her mother, the memories and happy tears spilled forth. Then Mary tried on each dress: the maternity dress her mother had worn the day Mary was born, the dress she had worn to Mary's piano recital, the dress she wore to her twenty-fifth anniversary party. With each dress came stories, incredible, rich stories that wove the fabric of a life. At the end of the day, the garments were returned to their plastic shrines, and Mary kissed her mother good-bye for the last time.

A New Marriage Ritual

I think my favorite ritual was around getting married," visual artist Carole Rae remembers.

I really wanted to be with one mate. I wanted my son to have a father. I wanted to center. I decided I needed to be clear about what my values were and then say them to my friends in a very clear way. Then I could proceed in a new direction. I decided to marry myself.

I asked a Zen priest and his wife to act as priest and priestess, and together we created this ritual of marriage to myself. First I read my vows and then did a traditional Japanese tea ceremony in this little teahouse. It was a very powerful thing to do. It was like clearing the way so that I could actually find a real partner. After that ritual it took me six months until I found my mate, Watanabe.

When Watanabe and I got married, as part of our wedding ceremony he married himself. First he came down the aisle at the Conservatory of Flowers in San Francisco by himself and said what his personal values and vows were.

Then we came together with our guests and built a house out of paper parts—paper windows and bamboo structural parts—and each guest carried part of this house. The words of our ceremony were about actually building our house and creating the river because Watanabe means "the place you go to cross the river." It was really fun and very special. It wasn't like a wedding where everyone is slightly nervous or anything. It was all our friends gathered together to help build this shrine that we stood under to exchange our vows. We were ecstatic.

School Days

The night before school starts each year, storyteller/performer Kate Luna lays out her son's new school clothes and lights candles for each year of school he has completed. School pictures from previous years are brought out, from kindergarten's chubby grin to "rad" fifth-grader. Old pages of schoolwork, showing progress from early attempts at writing the alphabet to cursive essays and long division, are displayed. A crystal stands beside each candle, and as each is lit, her son makes a wish.

"This year I want to get to pitch, get really good at math, do some poetry . . ."

Kate also uses Halloween as a way to remember the sacredness of life and all those who have passed on. Alongside pumpkins, dried gourds, and festive decorations, Kate and her eleven-year-old son look through old photographs of friends and relatives long gone, as well as the "newly gone." "Dog pals and cat friends are my son's additions," Kate says, smiling. A feather is placed for the bird that hit the window. Memories and stories are shared. Time is taken to be grateful for life and to remember those who have died.

When Salli's daughter, Sasha, was a toddler, they would go to the ocean every day, no matter what the weather was. It was their special time to be together. One day Sasha became very angry over something. Seeing her frustration, Salli began to lightly stamp her foot in the hard sand near the water's edge. Sasha began to imitate her mother. Salli stamped harder and so did Sasha. Soon they were stamping and laughing, making bigger and bigger circles as the water made deep muddy slush pockets around them. Pretty soon Sasha forgot all about whatever it was that had made her mad. She was in control, having stamped out her own anger. Salli recalls, "After that, whenever either of us would get mad, we would begin to stamp our feet, and soon we were laughing and our frustration was forgotten."

Touchstones

Kat Harrison is an ethnobotanist who spends a lot of time at her gardens in Hawaii and Peru when she's not attending seminars around the country. She knows that ritual plays an important part in keeping her family close. "I have certain small practices. When I'm in one place and not on the road, I light a candle every evening at dusk, and if there's anyone of my extended family and friends who is in trouble or needs healing, I take a photograph or an object of theirs and I light a candle and I send them energy. I just thank the world for being here and for being in it. That's really a very good touchstone for me everyday. I'm trying to teach my children that too."

It's Your Turn

Often we get swept up in celebrating special events in ways that are no longer appropriate but have become habit. Everyone has opportunities to create their own special occasions for joy and celebration; rituals that mark beginnings and ends. Authentic rituals help make sense out of our lives. They are both meaningful expressions of our individual inner lives and significant touchstones within our communities.

Here are a few questions to consider as you reexamine the role ritual plays in your life:

What rituals have you kept over the years?
What rituals did you grow up with that no longer serve you?
What, if anything, do you want to happen on your birthday?
Thanksgiving?
Fall Equinox?
Christmas?
Chanukah?
Earth Day?

Are there traditional holidays that feel empty and no longer give pleasure? Are there certain times that are special to you but not generally celebrated? Are there big bash celebrations that you would rather spend alone or with just a few good friends?

EXERCISE

List the times of year that are special to you—holidays, special anniversaries like marriage, surviving a life-threatening event, death of a loved one, changing of the seasons, etc. Write down how you would like to honor that day, how you would like to spend your time. What would you have to do to make these occasions happen?

Like Robert Brent, who had no guidelines to follow but his own desire to acknowledge his son's transition to manhood, we can invent whatever ritual we want in our lives. In doing so, we not only honor a moment in time, but create something lasting and memorable for ourselves and those we care about.

By taking these opportunities to create heightened experiences of joy, reflection, and memory, these celebrations become important touchstones in our lives. By reconnecting with our community and the earth through ritual, we will deepen our lives and fuel our creative fires.

The Magic of Storytelling

Some people think we're made of flesh and blood and bone. Scientists say we're made of atoms. But I think we're made of STORIES! When we die, that's what people remember, the stories of our lives and the stories that we told.

—RUTH STOTTER

There is a storytelling renaissance underway in America. As a society, we need the healing and connection that comes about through storytelling. Storytelling is an important and magical vehicle for bringing people together and for passing along what's important in a culture. Stories are avenues to the spirit. They are a wonderful way to transmit our deepest values and to connect with each other. And whatever we do to strengthen those golden links between one another nourishes us and brings more joy into our lives.

Ruth Stotter, a professional storyteller, believes each of us can make a difference and uses her craft to inspire others to do so. "I like to think I spread compassion and critical thinking through my storytelling. Storytelling is one way you can get people to care. If they can step inside the soul or wear another's moccasins through the story, then they can get that experience. I think stories are healing physiologically and psychologically. They are illuminating as well as entertaining. Stories give you alternative ways to deal with your life.

━━━━━━━━━━━━━━━ **EXERCISE** ━━━━━━━━━━━━━━━

We are all storytellers, but most of us are just not aware of it. To become aware of the stories you tell and your favorite personal stories, keep a small notebook with you and jot down the stories you tell your friends, relatives, and co-workers. Do this for at least a week. Jot down the story subject and the reaction to the story.

Joanie Sutton entertains and teaches children through storytelling. "I feel very close to my own childhood and try to give the children what I loved the most when I was a child," Joanie explains.

> Storytelling is an ancient magic considered a blessing from the gods. It's one of the first forms of entertainment. It's not the same as watching TV or listening to a tape recorder or going to a movie. There is some kind of personal bond that is set up between the storyteller and the audience that has an incredibly hypnotic, healing quality to it. Being one myself and doing it everyday, I still can't tell you what that magic is. It's like I've stepped into the river of an ancient tradition. I have the honor of being in that river for my lifetime, and then after I die that river will go on and someone else will be in it.

Storytelling is not only one of the most ancient human rituals, it is one of the easiest to get into for the ritual-shy. Although Joanie Sutton and Ruth Stotter are professional storytellers, that same healing, bonding, and the passing on of tradition and values is available to everyone.

"Family stories are wonderful ways of passing down who you are and where you belong in the world to your children," Joanie believes.

> Fathers sometimes tell stories to their kids when they go to bed at night, and many of them have come up to me and said the stories they tell their children often have stock characters that occur over and over again. I think

what these fathers are doing is taking certain characteristics of the children or of themselves and fictionalizing them or archetyping them into the storytelling mode. There is something extremely comforting for the children to hear their fathers expressing these inner feelings in this story way. Especially when they are going to sleep at night. Some of these men didn't even know they had this in them until they had children, and something deep was called up in them that they wanted to express.

Storytelling has become a very important part of Padi's family life. She even used storytelling to wean her first son from a bottle—by creating the "Bye Bye, Ba-Ba" story, a little homemade book about how when babies grow up and get teeth they no longer need a bottle.

"I read this to him every day for the two weeks before weaning him," Padi says. "The book also involved a ritual of hiding and finding the bottles, putting them in a bag, and actually throwing them into the dump while we sang this little song: "Bye bye, ba-bas, bye bye, ba-bas, bye bye, ba-bas, it's time to say good-bye." It worked great! By creating a ritual and a story, we helped our son make the transition to toddlerhood quite gracefully."

EXERCISE

Become a story collector. When you hear a good story, jot it down. Padi categorizes her stories by subject matter to use in her workshops and speeches. Salli, who is learning to write fiction, has a file folder full of personal stories scribbled on napkins and the back of envelopes. You don't have to be a professional speaker or a writer to collect stories. Everyone has plenty of opportunities to tell a good story to entertain, communicate, persuade, or enlighten. We all hear stories every day that move us but, like dreams, are easily forgotten unless an effort is made to capture them.

Padi and her husband share their love for storytelling beyond their immediate family:

Last Thanksgiving, we asked everyone to bring a story with them to tell after dinner. It could be any type of story: humorous, sad, an unusual experience. After the meal, we all moved into the living room and sat around in the ancient circle and told stories, one at a time. It was incredible. The stories were powerful, funny, poignant.

But what was even more special was the fact that we were all listening to each other at the same time! It was the best Thanksgiving we ever had.

One of my favorite stories from that evening was told by my Aunt Selma, who is eighty-four years old, tiny and frail, and who lived most of her life in a small apartment in New York. She led a rather quiet, sheltered life as a homemaker and wife. And, although we never thought of her having too many crazy adventures, not to mention doing anything out of the norm, she shared one of the best stories we heard that day—one that she had never told us before.

It seems that Aunt Selma and a friend had attended a funeral on a chilly autumn day. They had gotten a ride to the cemetery for the service, as there were no convenient bus or subway stops nearby. When the service ended, all the mourners left, forgetting that my aunt and her friend needed a ride home. When the women finally realized their ride had left, there was no one left except the hearse driver, who kindly offered them a ride. Not seeing any other choice, my aunt and her friend accepted his offer and got into the long, shiny, black symbol of life in the last lane.

On the way home, my aunt realized she needed to pick up some groceries and asked the driver if he wouldn't mind dropping them off at her neighborhood market. "No problem," he said. When they arrived, he graciously got out of the hearse to open the door for them, to the shock of a crowd of shoppers who couldn't believe their eyes. My aunt said it was the most memorable shopping trip she ever took!

From now on, when we do Thanksgiving at our house and people ask what they can bring, I know what to tell them: Bring us a story; bring us the gift of *you!* Your truth, your lessons, your life!''

EXERCISE

Organize your next social gathering around storytelling; a potluck party, a family get-together. Having everyone bring a favorite story to tell—anything goes! Prepare yourself for an especially powerful and memorable event.

Make sure everyone is willing to be respectful and listen—there should be no side conversations or interruptions during the telling. In many cultures, the storyteller shouts out a signal for the audience to respond to as a way of making sure they are ready to give their full attention. In Haiti, for example, the teller says "Cric" and only when she hears a unanimous and enthusiastic "Crac" from the audience, will she begin weaving her magic.

Some of our fondest childhood memories are of stories told around a campfire or at slumber parties after the lights are out. And what could ever take the place of a bedtime story? Storytelling doesn't have to be just a fond memory from childhood. It can be used throughout out lives to stimulate our creativity and bring us closer together.

EXERCISE

Here are some questions to stimulate your memory for stories to share, or to use as a fun game or party activity to stimulate others' stories. Write these questions out on a slip of paper, fold them up, and put them in a bag; let participants select one at random. This is also a favorite in business settings, such as corporate retreats and training ice-breakers.

- ◆ What was the best idea you ever had?
- ◆ What is the naughtiest thing you ever did as a child?
- ◆ What awes you and why?
- ◆ Tell us about a time you were frightened but everything worked out fine in the end.
- ◆ Tell us about one of the happiest times in your life.
- ◆ Tell us about a surprise you once had.
- ◆ What is the most bizarre coincidence you ever experienced?
- ◆ Share an embarrassing moment.
- ◆ Tell us a fond memory from school.
- ◆ Who influenced you the most while growing up?
- ◆ Decribe your first car.
- ◆ Tell us about the strangest date you ever went on.
- ◆ Describe the best or worst boss you ever had.
- ◆ What is the funniest thing you ever did or said as a kid?

To learn about storytelling festivals held throughout the country, order storytelling tapes, or find out more about the storytelling movement, contact the National Storytelling Association (NSA) at P.O. Box 309, Jonesborough, Tennessee 37659, Phone: 800-525-4514.

16

Stay on the Joy Track

Reach high, for stars lie hidden in your soul. Dream deep, for
every dream precedes the goal.

—PAMELA VALUE STARR

The path to joy comes from creative expression. When you
make the time and space to harness the energy in your life,
you can begin to express your unique creativity. Your joy will
increase. Your confidence will grow. Your life will be transformed. You will be living your life out loud.

It's now time to design your life-plan to help you get on the
joy track and stay there. This chapter is all about doing it! This
is where you pull together all you have learned in the preceding
chapters to make your personal action plan. Designing your
personal blueprint for unleashing your creativity and putting
more meaning and joy in your life is not only fun; it works.

As you've seen, there are many distractions and obstacles
on the path to living your life out loud. The primary key to
staying on track is very simple—set goals to make sure you stay
focused on getting what you really want.

Goal setting may not sound very exciting to you if you've
never done it before, but as successful people will tell you,

240

nothing works better for helping you stay on track and accomplishing what you set out to do.

The best way to stay focused on your goals is to write them down. Research has shown that only a tiny percentage of the population writes down their goals, yet writing down what you want is the most effective way to get it.

Writing down your goals will make you focus, and keeping them in front of you will ensure that you move closer to them every day. Many people resist making goals because they feel they'll change. Don't worry about that—your goals *should* change, and there's no rule saying you can't update them. In fact, we believe in annual and semiannual goal setting because your goals and dreams will change and grow, like they're supposed to.

Let's get started formulating your goals right now. Do the following exercises with the perspective that these are your goals right now, they're not set in cement. You can and should revisit them often so you can add, delete, or revise them. Look back on your 10% list as a reminder of what you want to focus on in your life, what really matters to you now.

What we think or what we know or believe is, in the end, of little consequence. The only consequence is what we do.
—JOHN RUSKIN

The main purpose for setting goals is to take the perfect life you envision and create a plan for making it happen. The following Life Balance Wheel exercise is one that our clients have given a four-star rating.

EXERCISE

Let's take a moment to examine how you feel about the seven major aspects of your life right now:

1. Your inner self (emotional, intellectual and spiritual development)
2. Your outer self (physical health, sexual well-being, satisfaction with your body image)

3. Your social self (relationships with friends, community involvement, service)
4. Your family (immediate and extended)
5. Your creative self (your hobbies, creative expression)
6. Your work
7. Your finances

On the chart on the facing page, you will be asked to graph your satisfaction in each of these areas by drawing a line around the circle. Complete satisfaction would be a line drawn at the outer edge of the circle. The less satisfied you are, the closer your line should be to the center.

First, look at an example from Margot, a workshop participant who loves her career as a private school administrator; her graph shows that she is 100% satisfied with her work. Being divorced for a year and just having begun to date again, her chart shows that she is 50% pleased with her social self. Because the divorce took a great financial toll on her life, she is very unhappy with her financial situation. The other aspects of her life are graphed as well.

Now it's your turn. Think about your satisfaction in each of the areas below and graph them accordingly.

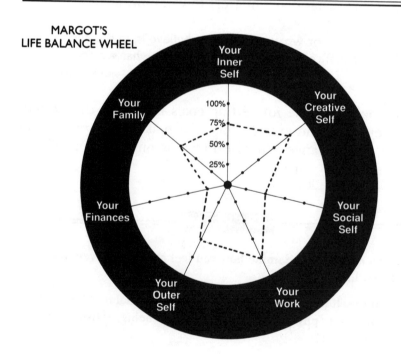

MARGOT'S
LIFE BALANCE WHEEL

YOUR
LIFE BALANCE WHEEL

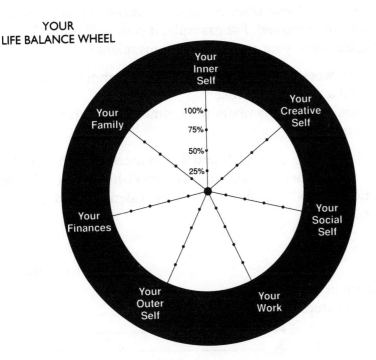

Perfection would look like a large perfect round wheel. Because everyone's life is always changing, we've never seen anyone's Life Balance Wheel look perfect. The purpose of this exercise is to be aware of where you are now and where you want to be in the future. Your goal is to work toward balance and wholeness in each of these critical life areas.

In each of the life areas, write a one-sentence description of what you would like to change or improve, as if it has already happened. Include how you feel about it. For example, let's say you want to start painting, but haven't made the time to pursue your interest. Your descriptive sentence might read: "I am painting two hours a week and loving it." Or if you are unhappy with a dead-end job and want to start your own business, your description might read: "I am now self-employed and feeling fulfilled and excited about my future." Make sure you state the description in a positive way.

Usually it's not enough to write down your goals; it's necessary to think through the steps you'll need to take to make the goal statements come true. Write down three action steps for each goal you identified. For example, if your goal is to relocate to a smaller town, your three action steps might be:

1. Take weekend trips to research new communities.
2. Find a real estate broker.
3. Write to the chambers of commerce in different communities.

Now, prioritize your goals and assign dates to each step. Be realistic about when you can best accomplish each step. Write the action items and dates on your calendar and pocket planner.

DATES TO COMPLETE

Your Inner Self: _____

Action steps: **1.** _____

                2. _____

                3. _____

Your Outer Self: _____

Action steps: **1.** _____

                2. _____

                3. _____

Your Social Self: _____

Action steps: **1.** _____

                2. _____

                3. _____

Your Family: _____

Action steps: **1.** _____

                2. _____

                3. _____

Your Creative Self: _____

Action steps: **1.** _____

                2. _____

                3. _____

Your Work: _____
   Action steps: **1.** _____
               2. _____
               3. _____

Your Finances: _____
   Action steps: **1.** _____
               2. _____
               3. _____

Then, write your goal statements on a three-by-five card, make some copies, and hang these cards where you will see them several times daily—on the dashboard of your car, on the door of the oven or fridge, on your bathroom mirror, in your workspace. How about a laminated version for your wallet, pocket, or purse! The point is this: When you constantly remind yourself of what is important in your life, you stay focused on it, and that focus brings you closer to your goals. You will find it easier to avoid distraction, procrastination, and getting sidetracked by everything that doesn't contribute in some way to reaching your goals.

Setting goals and reaching them can be done in many ways. We wanted to share this tongue-in-cheek story with you as a reminder of the importance of knowing exactly where you want to end up.

Padi goes one step further and, in addition to goals written on cards, keeps a notebook beside her bed, divided into the twelve months, with action steps to each goal written in the appropriate month. At the beginning of every month, she reviews the notebook as a reminder of what she plans to work on that month.

When you reach a goal, it's nice to acknowledge it in some way. Salli has always been a great believer in acknowledging other people reaching their goals and recently decided it was important to acknowledge herself as well. She loves stars and

THE BULL'S-EYE

There was once a nobleman who entered his son in a military academy to learn the art of musketry. After five years the son learned all there was to learn about shooting and, as proof of his excellence, was awarded a diploma and a gold medal.

On his way home from graduation he stopped at a small village to rest his horses. In the courtyard he noticed on the wall of a stable a number of chalk circles, and right in the center of each was a bullet hole. The young nobleman looked at the circles with astonishment. Who in the world could have been the wonderful marksman whose aim was so perfect? In what military academy could he have studied and what kind of medals had he received for his marksmanship?

After considerable inquiry he found the sharpshooter. To his astonishment it was a small boy, barefoot and in tatters. "Who taught you to shoot so well?" the young nobleman asked him. The boy explained, "First I shoot the wall. Then I take a piece of chalk and draw circles around the holes."

gives herself a gold star or sometimes two when she has reached a goal on her list.

Now that you have a clear picture of your current goals, let's look at ways to keep this list current. Once or twice yearly (depending upon how stable your life is and what stage you are in), we suggest taking a day of retreat and reflection to do this exercise to plan the coming year.

Some people enjoy doing this on their birthday. Padi and her husband take a weekend away each August and spend an afternoon during the getaway to do the exercise individually and to discuss their individual goals. They then combine their separate goals into a family goals list, which they keep handy and review regularly. They've even begun having their children set goals, as part of the family's New Year celebration. Their children, ages seven and ten, set simpler goals, since they don't concern themselves with finances, work, and inner selves. This year, for example, the ten-year-old's goals were: "Keep my room clean and neat, learn to type, improve cursive handwriting, and improve computer skills."

As a mother, Padi wasn't as concerned about her son's specific goals, but was more interested in the fact that he created goals, wrote them down, and is getting into the habit of goal-setting. The family reviews their goals together every few months after dinner to discuss each member's progress and remind one another of commitments made.

By writing your goals down, keeping them visible as a constant reminder of what really matters to you, and reviewing them regularly, you will find that the dreams you had only yesterday are coming true today. There is no faster or more effective way to get what you want and stay on the joy track!

Let's look a bit farther down the line. You've identified the areas of your life where you want growth to take place. The next exercise involves fast-forwarding your thinking to the *rest* of your life—long-range planning. At this point you may want to revisit the "How Much Time Do I Have Left?" chart on page 39. Take a moment and turn to that page now and remind yourself how many estimated days, years, and hours you have left on the planet.

EXERCISE

Make a Life Wish List of everything you want to accomplish, experience, see, and have for the balance of your life. Don't worry about the how and when, why and who. Just let your imagination soar. Make your list as long as you like. Be wild, bold, outrageous. Keep your judgment out of this exercise. Your ideas are like fire sparks, and when you judge them, you throw water on them! So, no matter how impossible or crazy your wishes may be, write them down. The wilder the better!

John Goddard was just a teenager when he overheard a friend of his parents' say, "Boy, I wish I were John's age again; I'd really do things differently." Hearing this made a powerful impression on him, and he vowed that he would not have regrets like this when he grew up. In the middle of his biology homework when the incident occurred, he took out a clean sheet of paper and began dreaming. At the top of the page he wrote *"My Life List."*

Number 1 was "Explore the Nile." #2 Explore the Amazon." #3 "Explore the Congo." As he wrote out his list, he visualized himself actually doing each activity: climbing Mount Everest, skin-diving, becoming an Eagle Scout, milking a poisonous snake, riding a bucking bronco.

His list grew to 127 items, and at last report, he had done 108 items listed and was working on the other 19. John Goddard's Life List turned out to be a treasure map of his entire life. By creating a list of his wildest dreams and acting on them, he has definitely lived his life out loud. Besides journeying to the most remote places in the world, he has flown a plane (#40), owned a horse, chimpanzee, cheetah, ocelot, and coyote (#94), and sky-dived (#82). Yet exciting adventures await him. Now in his seventies, Goddard's future plans include living to see the twenty-first century (#127), visiting the moon (#125), and composing music (#114).

How many items are on your Life Wish List? Take a few minutes now to add to it.

Keep this Life Wish List in a safe place and add to it often. It's a good list to refer to and revise *often,* since it reminds you of your wilder dreams! Use it to refer to when doing your annual/semiannual goal setting.

Setting goals and having a Life Wish List will keep you focused and on the joy track, but for good measure we have added some additional focusing tips used by some of the most creative and effective people we know:

- ◆ Have a personal theme for each year. Rick Gilbert, speaker and presentation skills coach, selects a central overall goal for each year. "Last year was 'the year of the new keynote speech,' while this year is 'year of the upgrade,' " he explains. "With a theme, ideas percolate in the shower, newspaper articles pop out, helpful books appear out of nowhere, people come into our lives that help us focus our new lenses. It is an amazing process," he says.
- ◆ Exchange your Life Wish List and goals with a planning buddy, or share with a mentor group. Agree to meet in

person or over the phone on a regular basis to check in on each other's progress. Knowing you have to report in on your progress is a great motivator. Getting regular support and feedback on your goals strengthens your commitment to them and helps propel you to make your dreams come true.

◆ Barbara Sanfilippo, motivational speaker, stays on track by using several techniques. For instance, she asks herself several times during the day: "Am I doing anything now that is diverting my attention from my priority goals?" Another technique is blocking out two to three hours each week specifically to work toward her most important goal. "I cross off the time in my appointment book," she says, "I don't allow any interruptions, unless they are urgent, and really focus all my energies on working toward that major goal."

Before going to sleep and occasionally during the day Barbara also visualizes herself reaching her goals. For example, one of her life goals is to someday have her own television show. She told us how she sees herself on the show, hears the camera people giving directions, feels the heat of the lights, and pictures the entire scene in great detail every time she flies home from a speaking engagement. "I memorize my goals every year," she explains, "and instead of writing them down, I constantly go over them inside my head."

◆ As psychiatrist Daniel Amen says: "Most people spend more time planning Christmas than they do their lives!" Take time each week to plan how you're going to spend your time. Most people find Sunday nights or Monday mornings a good time for planning the week ahead.

Every Sunday night, no matter what, Salli looks back over the past week and takes a few minutes to acknowledge what worked really well for her and what didn't and then plans the week ahead. It usually only takes her thirty minutes or so, and she feels it's an important addition to keeping on track. When you have your goals written down and handy, you can plug the action steps into your weekly "to do" lists as another way to stay on the joy track.

◆ Design a Dream Map. This is a collage of pictures cut out of magazines or illustrated by you that represents your goals. Barbara Sanfilippo showed us one she had created several years ago. On it were photos of romantic couples (she was single at the time and wanted to find a love relationship), pictures of the Greek islands (where she wanted to honeymoon), a beautiful home, a headline that said "New books" (she hoped to write a book someday), and a photo of a very successful woman. It was as if she programmed future memories, for indeed, nearly everything on her Dream Map has come to pass. She found and married a wonderful man, they honeymooned in Greece, she lives in a lovely home and was in the process of moving to an even more beautiful one when we spoke, she has authored a book and has another one on the way, and she has become a very successful speaker.

"It doesn't take any more energy to dream big than to dream small," Barbara says, "So why not dream big?" Even if you have no idea how to make the dreams come true, put them on your Dream Map anyway and let the universe figure out how to support *you*.

From being an artist I've learned nothing that you make is as important as the way you live your life. If the way you live your life is interesting, then the art you make will be vital. You can't make vital art without having a vital life. You can't fake art. The whole idea of living your life as an art form is more important than what you make. It's just taking time to be mindful of whatever it is you're doing and doing it beautifully. That's what nurtures you and the people around you. That's what makes your life feel good.
—CAROLE RAE

Joy is a choice you make. By making the commitment to unleash your creativity, you have chosen to increase the amount of joy you will experience in your life, as well as the amount of joy you bring into the lives of others. There is no one in the world at all like you. You are filled with wonderful gifts, as well as the seeds of great gifts. The world needs your creativity, and you need to share it with the world. By staying focused on your goals you will bring more joy into your life—and begin living your life out loud.

As our parting gift to you, here are the Ten Commandments of Creativity, highlighting the most important points we've discussed in this book.

**The Ten Commandments
of Creativity
for Daily Living**

1. Take More Risks
2. Listen to Your Dreams
3. Take Time Out
4. Simplify
5. Say No to the Conformity Monster
6. Say Yes to Fuzzy Boundaries
7. Trust Your Gut
8. Honor Your Goals
9. Play Often
10. Dance Your Dendrites!

Live Your Life Out Loud!

About the Authors

SALLI RASBERRY

Salli Rasberry is the author of six books and self-publisher of a best-selling book at the age of thirty. A pioneer in the fields of education and values-based business, she is a founding member of the Briarpatch, an international network of small businesses that incorporate environmental and social responsibility in their management practices. Salli has lived in a teepee, been a working partner on a sheep ranch, started an alternative school, was featured on the television series *Making Sense of the Sixties,* and is a visual artist. She was executive director of an internationally acclaimed environmental training center that launched the first worldwide environmental telecommunications network. Her friends call her Eco-Babe.

PADI SELWYN

Padi Selwyn is a popular international speaker and consultant on creativity and innovation. She is currently president of the Northern California Chapter of the National Speakers Association. Founder and former president of an award-winning advertising agency, she is also founding director of a northern California business bank; she is a newspaper columnnist, TV show host, world traveler, community volunteer, and daily napper. Known as the Entrepreneur Energizer, Padi has been creatively self-employed since the age of twenty-six.